George Charles Bell

Religious Teaching in Secondary Schools

Suggestions to teachers and parents for lessons on the Old and New Testaments,

early church history, Christian evidence, etc.

George Charles Bell

Religious Teaching in Secondary Schools
Suggestions to teachers and parents for lessons on the Old and New Testaments, early church history, Christian evidence, etc.

ISBN/EAN: 9783337003654

Printed in Europe, USA, Canada, Australia, Japan

Cover: Foto ©Lupo / pixelio.de

More available books at **www.hansebooks.com**

RELIGIOUS TEACHING

IN

SECONDARY SCHOOLS

SUGGESTIONS TO TEACHERS AND PARENTS

FOR LESSONS ON

THE OLD AND NEW TESTAMENTS
EARLY CHURCH HISTORY
CHRISTIAN EVIDENCES
ETC.

BY THE

REV. GEORGE C. BELL, M.A.

MASTER OF MARLBOROUGH COLLEGE

London

MACMILLAN AND CO., Limited

NEW YORK: THE MACMILLAN COMPANY

1897

PREFACE

THE following pages sufficiently explain their purpose; they are the outcome of a suggestion made by the Publishers, who considered that there was occasion for such a book, and that there were reasons for asking me to undertake it. But I have widely departed from the scheme which they suggested.

I have "taken my material where I found it," usually with careful reference to its sources; and one chief use of this short compilation will be to draw the attention of teachers to useful and accessible books, which have been freely used for it.

To their writers I must express my great obligations, as well as to friends who have given me help and counsel; especially the

President of Queens' College, Cambridge (Dr. Herbert Ryle); Archdeacon Sandford; Canon E. R. Bernard; Mr. George Macmillan; the Rev. H. F. Stewart (Vice-Principal of the Theological College, Salisbury); Mr. A. F. Hort of Harrow; and others. But I am solely responsible for what is found here; indeed, to some of these friends I am also indebted for kindly criticisms on parts of the MS., which lead me to offer a word of explanation on the following points.

(1) The short statement in Chapters IV. and V. of some results of the "Higher Criticism."[1] I am asked whether it is wise to invite the attention of young teachers to such information, and so possibly encourage its premature diffusion among pupils. In Chapter I. some reasons for this course are indicated. I may add that a wise teacher, recognising that education must be progressive, will not think it a duty to blurt out information indiscriminately, without due regard to the age and mental development of pupils. In good

[1] "Higher criticism" is concerned with questions of authorship and historical construction, as compared with criticism which has to do with the editing of texts.

teaching of any subject the "Law of Parsimony" must be observed. But for the teachers themselves, under the circumstances of our time, I am persuaded that some knowledge of the "more assured results of criticism," as applied to the Old Testament, is not dangerous but helpful to faith.

Among educated laymen perplexity about the Old Testament is not uncommon—an uneasy feeling that it is full of difficulties which debar discussion or exposition of it.[1] I have known cases in which a study of "the higher criticism" in books of various schools of thought, including the more advanced, has resulted, not merely in the removal of such perplexity, but in a fresh intelligent love and admiration of the Hebrew Scriptures.

Such study shows that throughout them, from Genesis to Malachi, witness is borne to God's love, mercy, righteousness, justice, wisdom; the several books uttering their testimony " by divers portions and in divers

---

[1] See the Rev. A. F. W. Ingram's *Old Testament Difficulties* (S.P.C.K.); brief answers to the more common and obvious questions.

manners." The teacher of the Old Testament has to disengage this testimony, to interpret it in simple ways adapted to young minds, to show its progressive development. And that he may be fitted for this work, that he may follow it on the right lines, without straying into irrelevance, he should from the outset look forward to the culmination of the teaching of the Old Testament in the Prophets, the Psalms, the Book of Deuteronomy; and then still further forward to its Divine interpretation and fulfilment in the Gospel.

The Divine inspiration of the Old Testament, its spiritual power, and its abiding influence on human character and destiny, will be fully appreciated only by him who recognises how it enfolds, even in its early pages, the germs of the fundamental ideas of the Gospel; how "the Law leads to Christ"; how He "fulfils the Law"; how "the testimony of Jesus is the spirit of prophecy."

Such intelligent study of the Bible is much helped by knowledge of facts about its historical development, such as are supplied by the reverent and sober teachings of the writers from whom the materials for Chapters IV. and V. are mainly derived.

(2) The omission of detailed reference to the history and formularies of the English Church. This is not because I undervalue the teaching of such subjects; it is indeed a cherished duty of my position. But outside the limits of the Church of England what is said in this book may be of use, whereas the inclusion of such special matter might limit its range.

In writing it I have had in view chiefly young masters and mistresses in "secondary"[1] schools of every type, who feel such difficulties as I have sketched in Chapter I., or (under the strong influences of examinations and text-books) are liable to overlook some of the main objects of religious teaching.

It may also be of some use to parents (especially of pupils in day-schools) who take part or interest in the religious teaching of their children.

---

[1] To avoid ambiguity, it may be explained that "secondary" education includes all between elementary (or primary) education and the Universities.

If these pages have any good seed in them, may God's Holy Spirit make it fruitful for His glory.

G. C. BELL.

P.S.—I had hoped to add a chapter on Christian Ethics, for which some materials were collected, but time failed for completing it.

MARLBOROUGH COLLEGE,
March 1897.

CONTENTS

		PAGE
1. THE DIFFICULTIES OF RELIGIOUS TEACHING IN SECONDARY SCHOOLS		1
2. THE RANGE AND SUBJECTS OF SUCH TEACHING		23
3. SUGGESTIONS ABOUT METHODS—		
A.—Lessons on the Old Testament		30
B.—The Inter-Testamental Period		63
C.—The New Testament		75
D.—Early Church History		89
4. THE INSPIRATION OF THE OLD TESTAMENT		97
5. THE COMPOSITE CHARACTER OF THE BOOKS OF THE OLD TESTAMENT, ESPECIALLY THE HEXATEUCH		129

6. CHRISTIAN EVIDENCES—

	PAGE
Introductory	131
A.—The Resurrection of Jesus Christ	134
B.—Miracles	139
C.—The Character and Teaching of Jesus Christ	151
D.—The Epistles of St. Paul	156
E.—Christianity and Evolution	159
F.—Evolution in History	163
G.—Christianity and Christendom	169
H.—The cumulative value of these Evidences	175
I.—The Difficulties of constructive Unbelief	177

CHAPTER I

THE DIFFICULTIES THAT BESET THE TEACHER OF RELIGIOUS KNOWLEDGE

THE teacher of religious knowledge has an aim different from that of teachers in many other subjects; instruction in grammar, mathematics, science, has for its object mainly the development of the intellectual faculties, memory, attention, reasoning power, etc.; but religious teaching is valueless, if it does not aim more at the heart than the head; its action upon the intellect must be subordinated to the primary object of stirring, lifting, purifying the desires and affections, so as to bring the heart and will into obedience to the will of God.

The ultimate aim of the Christian teacher is to lead his pupils to the Father through Christ, the Way, the Truth, and the Life, that they may grow up in the love of God and man. A subject such as this must be approached by a teacher with awe and reverence, a warning eloquently enforced by James Darmesteter,[1] who says, "Malheur au savant qui aborde les choses de Dieu sans avoir au fond de sa conscience un sanctuaire inconnu d'où s'élève par instants un parfum d'encens, une ligne de psaume, un cri douloureux ou triomphal qu'enfant il a jeté vers le ciel, et qui le remet en communion avec les prophètes d'autrefois." "The place whereon thou standest is holy ground."

In teaching children and young people it is of course necessary to lay a foundation of detailed instruction in the main facts of the history of God's revelation of Himself and His dealings with mankind, as recorded in the history of the Jewish and Christian Church; but always under the essential condition that instruction in historical facts shall be relevant and subordinate to the primary objects of religious teaching. Yet religious teaching is often degraded to the level of unintelligent history teaching; and there is perhaps no subject that can be taught so unintelligently as history. The mind may be burdened with

[1] *Prophètes d'Israel.*

facts, dates, details, and plans of battles, so treated as to be little more than a toilsome exercise of the memory; and after years spent upon such work the pupil may never have gained any clear ideas of the social and political lessons which history should teach. The religious teacher, recognising that instruction on such lines is utterly inadequate for his main purpose, will value the facts and details of Bible and Church history in proportion to their fitness for teaching and illustrating lessons of religion and morality.

"The true value of religious education is to supply children with that faith in man's destination for a spiritual life which nothing can give them except a belief that the universe is under the guidance of a Divine all-powerful Spirit. Without such belief man drops into a utilitarian secularist. We need then to use specially for education such parts of the Bible as display the highest qualities of human character developing under the influence of a pure faith, and thus foster the germs of spiritual heroism and earnest devotion."[1]

But in this, as in other subjects, teaching must be graduated according to capacity. In the religious teaching of young children, as in

[1] *Spectator*, February 1896.

other subjects, their quickness and freshness of memory will be turned to account by making them learn facts and details suited to their intelligence; but the primary aim will be to select and use facts and details as means of quickening and cultivating the germs of religious and moral feeling; towards God, love, reverence, trust; towards man, such emotions as are stirred by the biographies of the Bible. The purity and magnanimity of Joseph, the piety and wisdom of Samuel, the manly faith and religious earnestness of David, the heroism of Stephen, the unselfish zeal of Paul, and, far above all, the ensample of Jesus' most holy life, attract the fresh sympathies of the young, and teaching must indeed be dull which fails to draw from such sources that which stirs emotion and lifts the heart.

And in the early years this will be the main object and result of religious teaching; the reason is not much exercised; the higher ideas and truths of religion, sin, atonement, judgment, heaven, eternity, are as yet almost unintelligible, dimly foreshadowed by familiar types or analogies; the difficult problems of freewill, predestination, inspiration, have not as yet taken shape in the mind; the battle-cries of sects, baptismal regeneration, transubstantiation, infallibility of Pope, or Church, or Bible, are unheard or meaningless.

And thus it comes to pass that what is called "the religious difficulty" does not, or should not, exist up to the age when the reasoning and critical faculties begin to develop; until then the main difficulties of the religious teacher arise from the imperfections of his pupil's character and environment. But more serious difficulties begin to arise at the time when the young learner, in whose mind history, legend, and fiction have hitherto had indistinct lines of demarcation, begins seriously to ask, "Is it true?" No doubt this period may be delayed by laying on the mind at an early stage heavy burdens of rote work. It is as possible in this, as in other subjects, to transform the eager curiosity and interest of the child into the dull acquiescence of the fourth form boy, who will get up the history of the Old Testament or the Gospels with the same degree of interest and emotion as he expends on the campaigns of Caesar, or the reigns of the English kings. Such apathy may be more or less venial in the years when vital energy is largely absorbed in meeting the demands of physical growth; but when the young lad or girl begins to grow up into the young man or woman, education has to satisfy the growing demands of the reason. A wider field of knowledge is opening; history, literature, science, philosophy, present their suggestions and problems to the developing intellect, and the old question of childhood returns with quickened urgency, "Is it true?" The teachings of the Confirmation class may have awakened a sense of the personal living interest and reality of religion; facts and ideas hitherto passively or trustfully accepted suggest "obstinate questionings," and the young mind must endeavour to co-ordinate and reconcile them with the fresh knowledge that is streaming in from every side.

During this period of intellectual awakening the difficulties of the religious teacher are progressively increasing. If he is a mere literalist, with a compact logical system, he has only to deliver his message to his pupils, whether they will hear or whether they will forbear; and if they escape from the cramping narrowness of his system into the freedom of scepticism, he may still feel that he has done his duty according to his light.

It is otherwise with a teacher who has learned that religion is full of mysteries, imperfectly grasped by even the most mature intellects, and that the gift of God's revelation of Himself is conveyed in earthen vessels of human fallibility, so that the purest of human systems are, after all, only approximations to the "eternal verities." He is conscious that he has reached his own standing-ground of faith through mists and quicksands of doubt and perplexity, and that even yet at times it seems to heave and shake under his feet. And then, as he looks at his young pupils, he recognises that, even as God led man to Christ through gradual stages of revelation, so the individual mind must be educated progressively; milk must come before strong meat, and there must be a certain "economy" in religious teaching.

But what practical steps is he to take? Let us suppose a senior class of young lads or girls whose intellectual powers are being developed and stimulated by the subjects of a higher liberal education; they are being taught to think; they have in their hands the masterpieces of ancient or modern literature; they are becoming acquainted with the philosophic scepticism of Euripides or Lucretius, with the rationalism of Thucydides, with Goethe, Heine, Voltaire. Their critical faculty is stimulated by discussions on points of history, textual criticism, etc.; they are encouraged to take interest in the books and questions of the day; there is no censorship or "Index Expurgatorius" which shall debar them from theological or agnostic discussions in the magazines, or from the unorthodox speculations of Robert Elsmere or Trilby. In proportion to their intelligence, their love of truth, and their interest in higher things, they will eagerly read, and perhaps discuss among themselves, speculations on fundamental points in the pages of books or periodicals.

Meantime the religious teacher has to take them through a course of Scripture history, appointed for the term, and to be tested by an examination. His subject is the Book of Judges; he comes to the history of Samson; if he followed his own inclination he might pass it by, or take refuge in generalities, or say with the Scottish minister, "This is a very difficult subject; let us, my brethren, look it boldly in the face, and pass on." But in the supposed case none of these courses is possible; the book has to be "got up," and in the course of getting it up, some of the pupils will ask themselves, or each other, "Is it true?"

The teacher in such a case has a choice of

courses. He may reverently and discreetly set before them a view of "inspiration" less literal and mechanical than the old traditional theories, and teach them that the writers of the books of the Bible were enlightened and inspired in varying degrees, and that national or local traditions may have been incorporated into the early history of the chosen people.[1]

In taking this course, certain dangers must be seriously considered, and carefully guarded against. Such meat may be too strong for the immature; after the fashion of disciples they may follow their teacher's method further than he intended, so that the effort to lay secure foundations for a reasonable faith may undermine the structure of their belief. Again, some of the pupils may not have reached the stage of inquiry and speculation; so that discussion and criticism of what they have been taught to believe implicitly may shock them (and perhaps their parents), and lead them to regard with suspicion and distrust the teaching that was intended to guide them to a more intelligent belief.

Another course is to keep to the text of the book; have it "got up" carefully, with special attention to names and dates,

[1] *Cf.* Chap. IV. p. 108 ff.

geography, and illustrative detail, so that they may be well prepared for the conventional examination paper. For this course of instruction the ordinary manuals of Bible history are well adapted; they abound in examinable details, but they give little indication of differences in the value or inspired authority of different parts of the Bible. They cover all with an even surface of comment or paraphrase, even as a plasterer puts a uniform coat of stucco over some old wall, concealing alike the Roman tiles in the basement, and the medieval arch that was filled in with bricks in Queen Anne's reign.

Such a course of instruction and examination is far simpler than the other, and apparently much safer. Yet it is open to far graver objections. In the first place, this instruction has not really been religious teaching; it has been a teaching of facts from which the vital spirit has evaporated. Moreover, little or no provision has been made for the pupil's further development in religious thought and knowledge. Perhaps the docility of early years, and the personal influence of the master, may for a time restrain and defer inquiry into the questions inevitably suggested to the growing intellect by the sceptical temper of modern society. But there are grave risks in thus delaying the first steps towards the reconciliation of faith with reason. The young pupil passes from the schoolroom into the freedom of a university, or of social and professional life. The fabric of religious history and doctrine that has been reared in his mind is hollow and unsubstantial, liable to succumb to the first shocks of objection, argument, or ridicule.

There is, however, very serious practical difficulty in deciding at what stage in education, and by what methods and agencies, the teacher should begin to supplement instruction in the letter of Bible history and doctrine by a gradual unfolding of the principal arguments and objections that will ultimately have to be faced. There are two questions of first importance on which such supplementary teaching seems to be necessary: (1) the historical truth, and degree of inspiration, of the various parts of the Bible, especially the Old Testament; (2) the evidences of the Christian religion, *i.e.* those facts and arguments which convince an educated Christian that his faith is intellectually and spiritually more tenable than any of the rival theories of belief or unbelief that prevail in modern society.

It may be said that questions of such difficulty are premature in school teaching, and are rightly deferred to a later stage of development. The answer is that if at least the elements of systematic teaching on such subjects are not presented to our pupils before leaving school, in such a form as to encourage further study and inquiry, the majority of them will never find or make the opportunity of entering upon such study; there is great risk that many will lapse into the apathetic agnosticism that is not uncommon among the educated classes.

It is already obvious that the religious teacher's task is beset with difficulties inherent in the subject; there are others not less serious arising from imperfect qualifications in the teacher. Such difficulties, of course, impede teaching of every kind; still arithmetic or Latin may be fairly taught without a deep conviction of the value of science or literature; but if a man lacks conviction of the value of religious knowledge, he is peculiarly disabled from teaching it adequately; he may, indeed, impart knowledge of facts, but he cannot impart that without which the facts are comparatively valueless.

There are some who, having taken up school work with an honest sense of responsibility, and a faithful purpose to do their duty to their pupils, are yet conscious that they have themselves no sure standing-ground of faith; they can accept or acquiesce in the Bible and Christianity so far as to feel justified in undertaking "Divinity lessons" if required, but they are conscious of a certain haziness about the truths and doctrines of revelation, and the authority of the inspired books; and they are too honest to make a false show by affecting that which they do not fully believe. They are in that "twilight of belief" which makes a man unwilling to speak to others about truths of which he is half doubtful, while he is too conscientious to inoculate his pupils with disbelief or doubt or critical theories which, for lack of time or interest, he has not himself investigated. He takes up his "Divinity lesson" with mingled perplexity and uneasiness, and instinctively seeks refuge in details of Jewish history, geography, scenery, antiquities, and a variety of illustrative matter. Such instruction does not compromise; it can arouse and retain the attention of young people at the age when they have an eager appetite for facts, especially if they are enlivened by lively narrative and illustration. But such teaching has little to do with religion; it does not stir the heart, or affect character and conduct; it tells nothing of "the deep things of God." In fact, the teacher, not having life in himself, cannot impart it to others, and, with the best intentions, he fails, and is sometimes conscious of failure, in the most important subject that he has to teach.

This book does not profess directly to offer "aids to faith," or definite remedies for such weakness or haziness of belief; it has no such ambitious aim. Yet those who are conscious of, and perhaps deplore, this serious defect may find here incidental suggestions that may be helpful to them. If it awakens in them any fresh thoughts about the width, and depth, and living interest of the most vital part of their professional duty, they may be stirred to further inquiry and study. One of its objects is to map out a course of religious instruction on practical lines, and to suggest methods and books which may point the way to a higher standpoint and a wider horizon.

There is also the teacher who, with little or no interest in the religious purpose of educacation, has entered on school work because it seems to him the easiest or the pleasantest way of getting a livelihood; if he is required to take a "Divinity lesson," he seems to himself to be "bowing down in the house of Rimmon." It is the most irksome and uneasy of his tasks; he would gladly be relieved of it; and this inward feeling he cannot permanently conceal from the keen observation of boys and girls. His pupils will not be strengthened in the faith; he is a cause of grave anxiety to all who are interested in them, and, whatever may be his personal estimate of the use or reasonableness of faith, he cannot rid himself of a shamefast sense that he is in a false position. How can he set himself right? He may be able to get exemption by exchanging "Divinity" for some more congenial work; he may decline to take a mastership where such exemption is not possible; and if he can thus get time for reflection, he may even come to recognise what is the highest and most sacred function of a teacher of the young, and seek God's help to qualify himself for it by inquiry and study. The references in this small book may furnish some hints and directions.

On the other hand, there are many who

have a steadfast and earnest belief in the Bible and in Christian doctrine; who are genuinely anxious that their pupils should be rooted in the faith, and that, as a chief means to this end, they should learn and love "the sacred writings which are able to make them wise unto salvation, through faith which is in Christ Jesus."[1] They would therefore spare no pains to make the Bible a living reality, by such comment, exposition, criticism, and illustration as are suited to the age and capacity of the young.

Half a century ago the course of such teachers lay plain before them; they had inherited traditions which were generally accepted and little questioned. Discussions about the authenticity of particular books, the inspiration of Scripture, the relations between religion and science, and kindred problems, had not yet pervaded the atmosphere of educated society. But now the perplexities of the Christian teacher are at least twofold; amid the Babel of controversy he has to decide (1) how far these discussions may or should affect the form and character of his own belief; (2) what influence they should or must have on his teaching.

[1] 2 Tim. iii. 15.

Specially worthy of consideration is the case of young masters and mistresses whose mind is sufficiently open to recognise not only the existence, but also something of the weight and force of the common critical objections to the traditional views in which they have been trained; while yet the pressure of work, the absence of leisure, the lack of trustworthy advice and well-informed sympathy, make it hard for them to get assurance as to the right course. Ought they to abide by the old received views and methods? Or has the time come when some modifications are demanded by the progress of knowledge and thought? Those who are in this state of uncertainty may welcome some suggestions offered for their guidance. These suggestions make no pretence to originality; much of the material for them is drawn from recent writings of English theologians at Oxford and Cambridge, whose reverence, moderation, and sobriety of thought is recognised even by those who are disposed to differ from some of their conclusions.

In the following pages it is proposed to indicate some points in which traditional views about the Bible, or conventional methods of religious teaching, seem to require and admit of modification; the most valuable feature of these outlines will be the references to the books (most of them easily accessible) from which the material is largely drawn.

Again, something may be said on the influence of examinations on religious teaching. An intelligent teacher will desire, at least in senior classes, to give instruction about the morality and theology of the Old and New Testaments, the character and work of our Lord, the doctrines of Christianity, etc. Such teaching may be of the highest value to pupils, but it is less suitable for reproduction on paper, and for testing by marks, than questions on history, geography, etc.; and classes taught on such lines may be at a disadvantage in examinations of the ordinary type. Such incompatibility between examinations and intelligent teaching may be in a certain degree inevitable. Nevertheless, it may be reasonably urged that there is much room for improvement in the ordinary type of "Divinity" examinations; for, whatever be the cause, it often happens that examination papers contain an undue proportion of dry bones—questions on unimportant names, insignificant details of history, etc. etc. There was an Oxford story of a *viva voce* examination, in which a perplexed undergraduate was asked in slow succession, " Who were the Emims? Who were the Zuzims? Who were the Zamzummims ? " There is a Cambridge story of one who expressed his surprise that a pedantic colleague could not give information on some small point—" I wonder you do not know it, it is so unimportant." This seems to be the attitude of some examiners.

The nature of the subject makes it impossible to remove this difficulty completely, but it may be palliated in various ways :—

(1) Teachers may be persuaded that if they limit their teaching strictly to that which is examinable, or to the range of the average examination paper, their teaching will necessarily be defective; so that they should either assign so much time to religious instruction as will enable them to supplement by higher teaching that which is necessary for examination work; or economise time and energy by excluding from their " Divinity " teaching much that is not relevant to its higher purposes.

(2) Examiners and Examining Boards may be enlightened as to the relative importance of subjects, so that they may lessen the difficulties of the teacher by ceasing to require

a knowledge of comparatively unimportant matters, and by arranging their papers so as to encourage as far as is possible the teaching and knowledge of higher things. It is worth while to make an effort in this direction, for examinations naturally exercise a strong influence on teaching; according as they are good or bad, they can do much to guide or misguide. There are some examinations of wide range which powerfully affect the character and limits of religious teaching throughout England, *e.g.* the Local Examinations, the examinations of the Oxford and Cambridge Board, and of the College of Preceptors, which between them give the tone to the class teaching in many hundreds of higher and middle schools. Those who have the control of such examinations incur a great responsibility for that which they do, or leave undone. Schoolmasters and schoolmistresses, acting through the various organised bodies which focus their opinion, might do much to raise the standard and improve the quality of " Divinity " examinations by appeals to the Examining Boards.

Possibly the theological faculties at Oxford and Cambridge might be persuaded to combine their influence with the view of introducing into the examinations conducted by these universities a more intelligent method and a higher standard. One obvious and simple reform would be to put "Divinity" on the same footing as history. The latter subject, as befits its dignity and difficulty, is usually examined by experts. Why should "Divinity" be combined with classical books, verses, critical papers, etc., and assigned to men who may have little knowledge of the subject, and little interest in it? Such an arrangement is unscientific; it deals inadequately with a weighty subject, and it tends to impoverish the teaching. The one argument in its favour is that it is a simple plan, moving on the lines of least resistance, free from the danger of "clerical dogmatism" and party opinion. But previous remarks tend to show that too great a price is paid at present for this simplicity and avoidance of danger.[1]

Another difficulty has been already referred to—the character and quality of the ordinary manuals and text-books. If what has been said on pp. 1 ff. is accepted as a fair outline of the aims of religious teaching, there is a great

---

[1] Some detailed suggestions respecting methods of teaching and examining will be found in Chap. III. *A* for Old Testament, Chap. III. *C* for New Testament.

scarcity of such books as satisfy those conditions. This statement is not made at random, but after a scrutiny of many of the text-books commonly used; and it may be supposed that the masters and mistresses of secondary schools take trouble to select the best books that are available. Such Societies as the S.P.C.K., the Religious Tract Society, etc., and the many diocesan organisations for higher religious education, might do much to raise the standard of school manuals by laying down the lines on which they should be constructed; the demand would quickly produce a supply. This book will suggest subjects that deserve their consideration.

CHAPTER II

THE RANGE AND SUBJECTS OF RELIGIOUS TEACHING IN SECONDARY SCHOOLS

THE arguments for the necessity of religious teaching in schools have been much strengthened of late years by observation of some results of purely secular systems of elementary education in France, and in parts of the British Empire. In England Mr. Herbert Spencer has widely influenced opinion by his philosophical treatise on education, but in discussing intellectual, moral, and physical education he assigns no place to religious teaching; indeed, there is no reference to any religious sanction; parents and teachers are to be guided by purely utilitarian considerations, and the main agency is the discipline of experience. But no system of education has life in itself unless it teaches the essential principles of religion, and their bearing on character and conduct.

Religion has been defined as being "subjectively man's conception of the highest law to which he is subject, and his feeling and action towards it; while its objective quality is determined by the character of this highest conception."[1] Christian religion and morality inherit that which was the most distinctive feature of Jewish morality; the teaching that the goodness and holiness of God are to be the types of such attributes in men.[2] Reversing the normal order of religious speculation, the Biblical writers start from the nature of God as an ideal, and test the life and character of man by relation to it; God's own Being is the rule of man's life: "Be ye holy, for I am holy." Departure from this ideal is rebellion and sin, and this idea is developed in Christianity: "Ye shall be perfect, as your heavenly Father is perfect" (Matt. v. 48). The God of Christians, as revealed first in the Old Testament, and then more fully by Jesus Christ, is good, righteous, compassionate, loving; therefore the religious man hates sin, loves goodness and justice, is sympathetic and loving.

The religious teacher, starting from such ideas of God and of the meaning of religion,

---

[1] A. M. Fairbairn, *Religion in History*.
[2] T. B. Strong, *Christian Ethics*.

will seek in the Old and New Testament materials for setting before his pupils the character of God, and its effect on the character of man.

The Christian teacher looks on Jesus Christ as the centre of the history of religion; all that goes before converges to Him, all that comes after radiates from Him. Books, subjects, details, are suitable for a scheme of religious teaching in proportion as they contribute to a fuller and clearer knowledge of (1) the preparation for the Gospel by God's providence and revelation; (2) the Gospel itself; (3) the results of the preaching of the Gospel. Books, subjects, details that do not contribute to such knowledge, however valuable and interesting in themselves, are not suitable; nay, the scheme itself is so wide and comprehensive that it is absolutely necessary to guard against diverting attention to irrelevant matter.

The following considerations may help to enforce this necessity:—

School education has to provide for the religious teaching of young people between ten and eighteen or nineteen. This range of age would include most of the pupils in preparatory, "public," and "high" schools. The time devoted to class teaching in this subject is usually two hours weekly for not more than thirty-five weeks in the year (allowing for examinations, holidays, etc.), *i.e.* in the nine years from ten to nineteen a practical maximum of $2 \times 35 \times 9 = 630$ hours. A good deal of this time must be assigned in the later stages to repeating, revising, expanding the elementary knowledge which has been more or less imperfectly apprehended in the earlier stages. Accordingly, in most schemes arrangements are made for junior and senior courses; in the latter the subjects of the former are taught more thoroughly and widely, and supplemented by others suited to more developed brains.

Plainly this maximum of 630 hours is already full short for all the subjects that should be included in a scheme of liberal religious education, viz.:—

    (*a*) The preparation for the Gospel, the history of the Jewish Church, the theology and morality of the Old Testament.

    (*b*) The preaching of the Gospel, the life of Jesus Christ, His revelation of the Father, and foundation of His Church.

(c) The results of Jesus's life, death, and revelation in
  (1) The growth of the Church in the Apostolic age (and later, if time permits).
  (2) Christian ethics, as shown in the Gospels and Epistles.

These subjects are plainly necessary for all.

Other subjects suited to senior classes, and intrinsically important, are:—

(d) Creeds, formularies, liturgies.
(e) Christian evidences.
(f) Some knowledge of the history of religion in England.

Even the most necessary parts of this scheme cannot be adequately taught unless time is carefully economised by the exclusion of all matter that is not closely relevant to the object of religious education.

Before proceeding to details it may be well to anticipate the objection that such a programme is needlessly comprehensive, because the education of intelligent people does not stop at nineteen, and much that is here included may be left for a later stage of development. In answer to this it may be said that in a very large proportion of cases *systematic* instruction in religious subjects comes abruptly to an end when the boy or girl leaves school. If school education has laid, or even traced, foundations for the knowledge of these subjects, and if also the teaching has been such as to awaken interest in them, there is some hope, or even probability, that this interest may carry the learner on to fuller knowledge. Otherwise the conditions of modern life and society are such as to make this further advance hopeless or improbable in average cases.

If the boy or girl has acquired no real interest in religious knowledge before leaving school, if "Divinity" taught in a narrow conventional way has failed to get a hold both on his heart and his intellect, the ordinary pursuits and distractions of secular business and society will soon absorb interest and attention; the ignorant scepticism or indifference of companions will insensibly undermine the rickety fabric of conformity to orthodox views; that which has been slightly prized will be readily abandoned, and, with little reluctance or regret, the young man or young woman will lapse into the apathy for religion, not unmingled with contempt, which is only too common in the educated classes.

The difficulty of obviating this danger is increased by the fact that not a few teachers, recruited from the ranks of those who have lapsed into such indifference, themselves lack interest in the "Divinity" which they are required to teach; and under such circumstances the inadequacy of religious teaching propagates itself from generation to generation of teachers and pupils.[1]

Experience has shown that it is quite possible to include all the subjects above suggested within the limits of a school programme; and that they can be taught fruitfully, so as not merely to awaken the interest of pupils, but also to supply them with such modest "aids to faith" as may in some measure prepare them to encounter the difficulties of belief which beset young people at or near the close of school life. It is worth while to spend labour on such teaching; respect, confidence, perhaps even gratitude, will be felt towards a teacher who shows that he has weighed and measured his reasons for belief in that which he offers to teach, and that he is anxious to give some clues for future guidance.

[1] *Cf.* Chap. I. pp. 12 ff.

CHAPTER III

SUGGESTIONS ABOUT METHOD, ETC.

A.—Lessons on the Old Testament

METHODS are determined by aims, as the choice of a path depends on the goal to be reached.

The Old Testament has been read too much as a history book; the history was written under divine guidance and inspiration for the main purpose of teaching religion and morality; but the historical detail has been too much regarded as an end in itself, whereas the chief aims and objects of lessons in the Old Testament should be:[1]—

1. To set forth what it reveals about the character of God in His relations with man;

---

[1] In writing the following paragraphs I have been greatly indebted to Professor Driver's Sermons on the Old Testament.

His holiness, justice, wisdom; His graciousness and lovingkindness; His desire that man shall love Him in return; His anger against sin, mingled with readiness to forgive the penitent; His fatherly guidance of His chosen people, and of individual souls, by blessing and chastening, through success and failure; His providential rule over the nations; His gradual preparation for the kingdom of God in Christ, so that Egypt, Phoenicia, Assyria, Chaldaea, Persia, Greece, in turn contributed to " prepare the way of the Lord."

2. To interpret and show the moral value and significance of the manifold examples of human action and character which the Old Testament presents; to show (as in the 11th chapter of the Epistle to the Hebrews) the power of faith and trust in God under every variety of circumstance; to lead the hearts and intelligences of young people to recognise the nobility, beauty, and attractiveness of the best men and women who were trained under God's discipline and law; to discriminate between the good and the evil in characters formed under a progressive moral law which, in its earlier stages, was imperfect and rudimentary.

3. To show the relation of the law to the

Gospel; how it was a "schoolmaster leading to Christ"; how "the testimony of Jesus is the spirit of prophecy"; how the fundamental ideas of the Gospel—sin, righteousness, redemption—are found in germ in the Old Testament, waiting for their fuller development; how the twilight of the old system is more and more irradiated by the distant dawn of the "Sun of Righteousness." The wise teacher will treat this branch of his subject broadly and intelligently, not laying undue stress on far-fetched types, strained predictions, and minutiae of detail. The prophets and men of old saw "in a mirror, darkly"; they "desired to see the things that we see, and did not see them."

4. To lead young people, according to their various characters and stages of development, to appreciate the value of the Old Testament for devotional purposes, showing how prayer pervades it from end to end; how it inculcates and gives examples of thankfulness to God, adoration of His greatness and glory, longing for His presence, and for communion with Him, faith and trust in Him, confession of sin and supplication for pardon, joy and gratitude for His mercy and grace; how the character and attributes of God, and His

relation to man, remain unalterably the same in all ages, and amid all the varying conditions of human life. From the Psalms, the Prophets, the more spiritual parts of the Law, and the lives of the Old Testament saints, the religious teacher will draw abundant material for lessons peculiarly suitable to the earlier stages of religious feeling and belief.

5. A subsidiary, but not unworthy, aim is to show that the books of the "Divine Library" are noble models of literature in a great variety of forms. "The bright, picturesque narrative of the historical books, the graphic, living reality of the biographical sketches, the sublime, impressive oratory of the prophets, the delicacy and brightness of the Hebrew lyric, all possess the peculiar charm and grace of style which entitles them to a high rank simply as literature among the classical works of the human intellect and heart."[1] Some twenty-five years ago Matthew Arnold, in his *Isaiah, the Prophet of the Restoration*, made an eloquent plea for the use of the later chapters of Isaiah as a reading book in elementary schools, though he characteristically dwelt most upon their literary value. Admitting all that

---

[1] Professor Driver, p. x.; Mr. R. G. Moulton's *Literary Study of the Bible*.

he says on this point, there are much more cogent reasons for imparting to young people so much of the religious teaching of the prophets as is within their compass.

This is a wide and comprehensive programme, yet it is such that even young children can follow the outlines of it, while more advanced pupils will be fully occupied in filling them in with relevant details. Still it is already so wide that we must avoid, as far as possible, enlarging it by supplementary matter that lies outside its limits.

Shall we then say nothing about the critical problems which for many years past have absorbed a large share of the attention of students of the Old Testament? That is a question that demands careful consideration.

On the one hand it is acknowledged that the "religious, moral, and devotional value of the Old Testament is unaffected by critical questions respecting the authorship or date of its various parts."

On the other hand its historical and evidential value may be seriously affected by such criticisms, and also (a point of great moment in the teaching of young people), those who adopt "critical" views are compelled to depart in a greater or less degree from the traditional estimate of the literal and verbal accuracy of some of the Scripture narratives. What line must they take in presence of young pupils?

The present period of conflict and discussion of the criticism of the Old Testament has some resemblance to the time, some fifty years ago, when debate was hot, and opinion much divided, about similar critical questions affecting the authorship and authenticity of the books of the New Testament. Plausible theories were then being advocated, with incomplete knowledge of the facts, which since then have been finally abandoned. At that time teachers would have been unwise in according hasty belief to unproved hypotheses; they would have done wrong if they had attempted to expound them to pupils. Even so now the wise and right course seems to be a certain suspension of judgment on many questions of Old Testament criticism, and a judicious reticence with regard to theories and hypotheses which have not yet been amply verified by facts and arguments.

This vague general statement requires some detailed examples and illustrations which may show what are the limits and boundary marks of the reticence thus recommended.

For instance, is the teacher bound to adhere to the traditional explanation of such Bible narratives as those of the Fall and the Flood ?[1] Is he to deal with them as inspired literal statements of fact, discussing and commenting on them as he would treat, say, a narrative of the battle of Hastings ? This is still the method adopted in many popular manuals. But this method can no longer be followed by a teacher who knows that sober criticism has shifted the conception of large portions of Biblical history to a different plane.

It is true that "the assured results of criticism" is a phrase that is often used with undue elasticity of meaning; nevertheless the more conservative defenders of the inspired truth of the Bible are prepared to admit that the early narratives of the Bible are partly based upon traditions, probably brought by Abraham[2] from the home of his fathers, some of which have interesting resemblances to traditions found in Chaldaean records; and that the inspiration of the Holy Scriptures is shown not so much in the letter of the record as in the purifying process which has transfigured and spiritualised the primitive traditions;[3]

[1] Chap. IV. pp. 108 ff.
[2] Bishop Ellicott, *Christus Comprobator*, pp. 70 *sqq.*
[3] Chap. IV.

and also in the selection of material in such ways as to point steadily and progressively towards a definite goal, the higher righteousness ultimately developed, and manifested in the more spiritual parts of the Old Testament.[1]

Such considerations are, however, not within the grasp of pupils of all ages; to scatter them broadcast among children would show want of intelligence.

In fact, three stages must be distinguished: (1) The knowledge, belief, or opinion possessed by the teacher; (2) that which may be imparted with caution and discretion to elder and more advanced pupils, say after Confirmation, if it is deferred till the age of fifteen or sixteen; (3) that which must be taught to younger pupils.

To the latter we must teach the facts as they stand on the pages of Scripture, not cramped and disfigured by any summary, analysis, or paraphrase, but in the simple beauty of the language of the English Bible. There are, no doubt, arguments in favour of the use of selections for junior pupils, while the study of the complete text of the Bible is

---

[1] Hermann Schultz, *Old Testament Theology* (translated by J. A. Patterson; the second volume is specially valuable).

deferred to a later stage; and there is no lack of selections that may be used with advantage, suited to various methods and principles of teaching (such as those of Miss Yonge, William Rogers in his *Children's Bible*, the Rev. M. G. Glazebrook, Dr. Stokoe). But in any case it is most important for every reason that from the first young people should grow familiar with the actual words of the English Bible.

They must learn about names, places, actions, the sequence of events, the marked features of character; but everywhere there must be such a discreet selection as shall winnow out details that will not help towards the fuller conceptions that will be within their range at a later stage. For the purposes of this elementary teaching it is useful to construct a scheme or framework of the several main periods of the Jewish Church, showing the religious and moral relation of each to those that precede and follow it. Such a scheme can be made so short and simple that even the youngest pupils may be made familiar with it by frequent repetition. It helps materially to an intelligent grasp of the history. Within this framework the outlines of Bible history and biography will be traced with judicious economy. These earlier outlines will resemble the practical maps, in which only such lines, names, and features are introduced as are of cardinal significance, in lieu of the well-intentioned but mistaken completeness of detail, which simply confuses and blurs the attention and the memory.

And even in the later stage there will be a discriminating avoidance of less important detail; the object will be not greatly to increase the mass of facts, names, etc., that have to be remembered; but rather to infuse life and spirit into the letter of the record by imparting to the more mature intelligence, to the more developed and deepened feeling, so much as it can assimilate of the moral and spiritual meaning of that which was learned in the more elementary stage.

For instance, in the earlier stage, from the first chapter of Genesis the young boy or girl will learn the Bible narrative of creation and of the "days," with their successive stages of development. In the later stage the pupil will be led to think of the meaning, the wonder, the glory of God's creative work; to see that the ancient story, though not literally foreshadowing the later discoveries of science, yet sets forth in sublimely poetic form the omnipotence, the wisdom, the loving providence of God, who has so adapted His marvellous works to the needs of man and the lower animals.[1] And, in connection with this, illustrations will be drawn from such later commentaries on the creation as are supplied by some of the Psalms (*e.g.* lxv., civ.), by passages in the Prophets, in the books of Job and Wisdom, in the words of our Lord, in the Epistles.

Just as a good edition of the Bible is furnished with the references which supply in themselves the most useful of Bible commentaries, so the teacher's notebook will be plentifully enriched with parallel passages which interpret scripture by scripture, and show not only the unity of the Bible, but the growing richness and depth of the thoughts which link together the writers of Holy Writ by the chain of Divine inspiration.

Again, in the third chapter of Genesis the younger pupils will read the letter of the narrative of the Fall—the serpent, the trees, the temptation, the sin, the judgment, the promise of ultimate victory. In the later stage it will be explained that it is not a literal record of historical facts, but an inspired

[1] Professor Ryle's *Early Narratives of Genesis.*

presentation of essential truths respecting temptation, sin, retribution, redemption; and, in connection with this, reference will be made to passages in later books, such as the Psalms, Proverbs, Wisdom, the temptation of our Lord, St. James, St. Paul in the Epistle to the Romans. Thus the story of the Fall, instead of standing isolated in the memory, to become in later years a perplexity, a stumbling-block, or an occasion for profane merriment, will be accepted and cherished as the germ of some of the deepest teaching about the most solemn and momentous realities of human life.

And plainly, if the main points of the Bible history are treated with similar fulness of exposition and illustration, the teacher will no longer have any inclination to waste precious time and energy on unimportant detail; he will pass from peak to peak of the Bible history by a high-level route. He will appreciate the relative importance of the facts, ideas, materials, methods, that are or can be utilised for Bible teaching; and the selection of that which is more intrinsically valuable will stimulate his own interest in " Divinity lessons," will awake in his pupils a vital, germinal, fructifying appreciation of the rich treasures of the Bible, and open avenues of access to higher truth, which will in many cases be followed up in mature life.

The necessity of such selection has already been more than once indicated; principles and methods of selection have still to be considered. It may be supposed that before going to the first school, say at the age of ten or eleven, a child will have learned at home outlines of the simpler narratives of the Bible, so as to know something of the history of Abraham, Joseph, Moses, Samuel, David, etc. This outline of knowledge the school course will supplement with further details. But the amount of detail in the books of the Old Testament is enormous and bewildering by its mass and variety. Of the three great volumes of the *Dictionary of the Bible* a large proportion is devoted to Old Testament history, biography, geography, etc. It is not possible, even if it were desirable, that young people should learn all indiscriminately; it would be a crushing burden for the attention and memory.

What principles of selection should be adopted? Is every fact in the history (say) of the Judges or of the Hebrew monarchy equally "profitable for teaching, for reproof, for correction, for instruction in righteousness"

(2 Tim. iii. 16)? From these historical books a Christian boy or girl should gather the main outlines of the history of the Jewish Church—that is, of the principal men, events, laws, and revelations, by which the chosen people were gradually trained and fitted to become the depositaries of the Gospel revelation.

It is not then necessary to learn details of the history of the nation which are relatively unimportant in their bearing on the history of the Church. These details are, no doubt, valuable to the student of history; to him nothing can be more interesting than the records of the marvellous nation whose destiny has been unique. But the religious teacher will be wise if he omits many of them, and selects only those which are useful for his special purpose; for there is urgent need of economy of time in order to find space for matters of great intrinsic importance. Under the present system it is common for boys and girls to know facts about insignificant persons and places, and yet to know practically nothing about the religious teaching of the Law, the Prophets, and Psalmists; or about the gospel of St. John; or the ethics of Christianity diffused through the Gospels and Epistles (except so far as they are included in various

Catechisms); or the influence of such men as Athanasius, Chrysostom, Augustine, on the history of the Christian Church; or the evidences of Christianity. It is full time to plead for careful reconsideration of the method of dealing with this important and difficult subject of Old Testament history. We have not done our duty by our pupils if we are content to cut the Bible from Genesis to Nehemiah into a certain number of approximately equal sections, and then to leave teachers and examiners to decide without guidance, by mutual action and reaction, what knowledge is to be required of boys and girls. There is urgent need of a more intelligent, discriminating, religious system of instruction in the Old Testament Scriptures, on such lines as are broadly traced in the preceding pages.[1]

Such parts of the history as are less pertinent to this purpose would then be omitted, or passed over lightly; there would be a careful sifting which would set aside (as valuable mainly to the student of Hebrew history), some parts of Genesis and of the other books of the Pentateuch, and much of the history of the Judges

[1] W. Sanday, *The Oracles of God*, pp. 118, 120-126; A. F. Kirkpatrick, *The Doctrine of the Prophets*, Lecture XVIII.

and the later historical books.[1] This economy of time would make it possible in the more advanced stages of teaching to give more attention to the religious and moral teaching of the Law[2] (especially the book of Deuteronomy), the Psalms, and the prophetical books; it should be possible even in a junior course to show in outline why these elements of the Old Testament Scriptures have a transcendent and permanent interest and value, which the fuller revelation of the New Testament has by no means abrogated or destroyed. "For all of us the Old Testament is a useful way of entrance into the New Testament. We never can understand the New Testament while we are ignorant of the Old Testament. It supplies, as it were, the alphabet, the letters, the simple thoughts in which the higher and deeper lessons of the New Testament are written. Nay, more, there is much about our life here on earth, as God would have it be, which is taught plainly in the Old Testament, and which is either not taught at all, or taught very slightly in the New Testament. Any one who tries to carve out for himself a

---

[1] See Appendix to Chap. III. A, p. 61.
[2] See Duncker, *History of Antiquity*, vol. i. pp. 387, 479, 484; ii. 202; iii. 24-29.

religion out of the New Testament will assuredly make something extremely unlike the true complete Christian faith."[1]

What has been said about selection, and the avoidance of irrelevant detail, may give rise to a misconception of its scope and purpose. The spiritual teaching of the Bible, especially of the Old Testament, is a subject by no means easy to convey to the minds and hearts of young people; it would be obviously futile to attempt to convey it in an undiluted, incessant stream of homiletic exposition; that would only produce weariness and disgust, or, at the best, what has been called " devout inattention." The Bible cannot be taught effectively to any one, still less to boys and girls, unless they are led to feel its reality, to understand that its books were written by and to real men in times as real and living as our own. Accordingly, in reading such parts of the Bible as are selected for class work, many kinds of illustrative matter (history, antiquities, geography, pictures, photographs, etc.) will be turned to account by the practical teacher; but always under the conditions that (1) such illustration shall be strictly pertinent, and contributory to the main purpose of conveying to his pupils the spiritual

[1] Professor F. J. A. Hort, *Village Sermons*, p. 141.

import of the book or passage selected; (2) the setting must not obscure or impair the jewel; the framework must not overlay the picture; from the lesson, or course of lessons, the spiritual teaching must stand out in central and pre-eminent clearness. Such teaching, if it is plainly seen to be the outcome of knowledge and conviction, will not fail to reach the heart and conscience, and stir interest and attention.

In considering criteria for estimating the relative value and importance of different books, or parts of books, of the Bible, the religious teacher will have to accept from others, or form for himself, judgments on some difficult and delicate questions of Biblical criticism. Few even of the most conservative students of the Bible (as distinguished from the average uninstructed reader) can now retain the opinion, not uncommon thirty or forty years ago, that all parts of the Bible are of equal value and authority; varying degrees of inspiration are now almost universally admitted.

Again, traditional opinions about the date and authorship of many parts of the Old Testament have been called in question, and some of them can no longer be considered to rest on sound foundations; criticism, history, archaeology have more or less recently discovered and established facts which make some of the old positions untenable. It is beyond the scope of this book to enter minutely into this subject, but the following questions may be mentioned as among the most important which have been either practically decided, or are still under discussion :—

    (*a*) The composite structure of the Pentateuch.

    (*b*) The relatively late date of the book of Deuteronomy and of other parts of " the Law."

    (*c*) Doubts about the Davidic authorship of many Psalms attributed to David, and the authorship of Proverbs, Ecclesiastes, and the Song of Solomon.

    (*d*) Doubts (or even definite conclusions) respecting the traditional date and authorship of the book of Daniel.

    (*e*) The ascription of the later chapters of Isaiah to one or more unknown prophets later than Isaiah.

It will be seen that in some cases, as in (*a*) above, an opinion on a critical question may be the basis of a principle of selection (as in the case of Mr. Glazebrook's books). In many cases criticism need in no way affect the teacher's estimate of the usefulness of a document for his special purpose. There are chapters in Deuteronomy, Psalms, passages of Isaiah, whose intrinsic value is in no way affected by questions of authorship; such questions may in such cases be rightly set aside as irrelevant to a school course.

And it may be added that young people care little about the date or authorship of the books that interest them; they will love and cherish their Bible in proportion as they are led to see and feel that it has a living interest now; they will be convinced of the essential truthfulness of the Old Testament history if they are led to see that it is the early source and foundation of some of the most vital truths in the world they live in. And to ensure this result the teacher in his class lessons will be carefully on his guard against a purely literary treatment of the books of the Bible.

But the teacher will naturally seek for himself further knowledge, more assurance of the quality and firmness of the ground on which he treads; it is, in fact, his duty thus to inform himself, both for the satisfaction of his conscience and intellect, and that he may avoid the vagueness which produces mistrust in his hearers. Reticence should be the result, not of haziness or ignorance, but of a deliberate, thoughtful choice between that which is and that which is not adapted to his class. For the benefit of those who may have small time or opportunity for independent study, or who have not easy access to sources of information, a slight sketch will be given later of some of the more important critical questions, with references to some of the most handy and accessible books.[1]

After knowledge of this kind has been acquired it will be necessary to decide in what measure, and at what stage, it should be communicated. The following suggestions are offered :—

If it is assumed that the junior classes will range from about 10 years of age to 15-16, and the seniors from 15-16 to 18-19, (*a*) the juniors will be taught simply the letter of the Bible, with such omission, compression, rearrangement, and grouping of materials as has been previously recommended ;[2] always with careful insistence on the religious features and aspects of the narratives, *e.g.* the Creation, the Fall, the Call of Abraham, the history of Jacob, Joseph, Moses; the Law, and especially the Decalogue (dwelling on the relatively high moral and religious standard

---

[1] See Chaps. IV. and V.   [2] Chap. II.

of the Jews as compared with their neighbours and with other nations of antiquity); Samuel and the beginnings of the prophetic order; Saul and David, the apostasy, Elijah and Elisha, the great reformations under Hezekiah and Josiah, the influence of the more important prophets (Amos, Hosea, Isaiah, Jeremiah, Ezekiel), the Exile, the Return.

It will be observed that this choice of topics implies very considerable omission of details now commonly included in "Divinity lessons" of quite young boys; but even so it is a large programme, which will require careful arrangement and judicious selection of the points most worthy of attention. Perhaps in this junior period as much time may be assigned to study of the Old Testament as to that of the New Testament; its standard of morality and religion has a certain affinity to that of young people (at any rate boys) up to their "years of discretion."

(b) In senior classes the staple of the work will, of course, be to complete and fill in the previous outlines of the religious and moral teaching of Scripture; but this may be supplemented by some elementary teaching about such questions as the origin and nature of the early narratives of Genesis; the composite character of books; the different documents of the Hexateuch (recognised in some degree even by the defenders of traditional views);[1] the re-editing and gradual accretion and compilation of the historical books, affording a reasonable explanation of many difficulties which give occasion for the more dull and vulgar objections to the Old Testament history; the evidences that God's revelation to His people was gradual and progressive, affording a solution of other difficulties. The character and permanent value of the religious, moral, and social teaching of prophets and psalmists will be more fully treated; and, with due discretion, something will be said about the character of the Divine inspiration of the Old Testament, to which it owes its unique power and influence on human progress in pre-Christian and Christian times.[2]

Much discretion will indeed be necessary in handling such questions as are still under discussion, and excite strong feeling among the upholders of conflicting theories. In what the teacher says about them to his pupils he will desire not to enlist them as

[1] Bishop Ellicott, *Christus Comprobator*.
[2] Much useful material for such teaching may be gathered from the *Cambridge Companion to the Bible*; see also Chap. IV.

partisans, not prematurely to encourage a critical spirit; but only to afford such information as may give a clue for their guidance through some of the more obvious difficulties of Scripture, and help them to form intelligent principles of interpretation, so that as they grow older they may be better qualified to " give a reason for the faith that is in them." He will always bear in mind that the main object of his teaching is to lead them to value and love their Bible. It has been compared to a great cathedral which was in building for some fifteen centuries. It was built for worship, holiness, devotion; for this it is not essential to know at what precise date each part was built, from what quarry the stones were brought, and what materials from older buildings may have been used in its construction.[1] It is essential to enter it with a reverent sense of the high purposes for which it was built, and a desire to be taught of God. Therefore the main point in the teaching of the Old Testament, while or after impressing the important facts on the memory, is to direct attention to the great moral and religious truths which are the essence of the Bible.

[1] Professor A. F. Kirkpatrick, *The Divine Library.*

It is in this point that some of the most popular manuals of the Old Testament are seriously defective; they give full and interesting explanations and illustrations of history, geography, ceremonial, customs, etc.; but the moral and religious truths are assumed or ignored; they are not drawn out and enforced. It may be that the writers assume that such enforcement may, should, and will be part of the teacher's duty; it may be that they keep their eye too steadily fixed on the requirements of examinations. Then the majority of teachers, guided by the text-book, and anxious about the examinations, are content if their pupils can reproduce the facts of Bible narratives, with the illustrations from history, geography, etc.; while the examiner thinks he is bound to limit his questions by the range of the ordinary text-books. Thus writer, teacher, examiner, each influenced by, and influencing the others, unconsciously form a kind of "triple alliance" for excluding from the teaching of the Old Testament just that which is most essential to it.

Now, when a large number of able and conscientious people combine to follow a course which is not the best possible, there must be some strong reasons for their action. In this matter they are obviously influenced by the difficulty (1) of effectively teaching moral and religious truths to young people in lesson hours; (2) of adapting such teaching to the requirements of examinations.

The conditions of the problem will be more clearly shown by giving a few specimens of subjects and questions which, if not included in text-books and examination papers, should at any rate find their place in the teaching; such as the following :—

1. For topics suggested by the early chapters of Genesis see Chapter IV.

2. God's covenants with men :[1] (*a*) with Abraham; its literal and spiritual fulfilments (the latter admitting of copious illustrations from the New Testament) : (*b*) with Israel in the Mosaic dispensation; its literal and spiritual fulfilments; its differences from the earlier " covenant of promise "; its gradual preparation for (*c*) the new Covenant of the Christian dispensation (Rom. iv.; Gal. iii.; Jer. xxxi. 31).

3. The characters of the chief personages in the Bible, and the qualities that God approves,

[1] In these pages, and elsewhere, I must acknowledge great obligations to Mr. C. G. Montefiore's *Bible for Home Reading*. I cannot, however, accept all his conclusions. The book is indeed written for Jewish parents from a rather advanced standpoint, but Christian teachers and parents may gather from it much that may be helpful.

encourages, develops in them; their faults and frailties indicating the truthfulness and honesty of the narrative, and showing their human naturalness: "they were tempted even as we are." Therefore, while we are warned to shun their faults we may be encouraged to imitate their excellences.[1]

4. The significance of Abraham's call, and of his obedience to it.

5. "The blessing of the nations" a prophecy not simply of the Messiah's advent, but of all God's revelation to the Jewish and Christian churches, and of its results in human history.

6. The sacrifice of Isaac, both a trial of faith, and an effectual discouragement of human sacrifice.

7. The selfishness of Jacob, Joseph, and his brethren, and the sorrow and suffering that resulted from it.

8. Joseph's later magnanimity and forgiveness, results of the discipline of trial and suffering.

9. The historical importance of the Exodus not merely to the Jewish people (illustrated by the frequent references to it throughout the Scriptures), but also to mankind at large.

10. Jewish ideas about the punishment of their enemies, characteristic of an early stage of morality and religion, not consonant with the nature of God as it was more fully revealed in later ages.

11. The teaching of Scripture in reference to

---

[1] See Dean Church's *Discipline of the Christian Character*.

the bondage in Egypt, and the deliverance from it; inculcating justice, charity, consideration for others; and also thankfulness to God and self-consecration; connection with Christian ideas.

12. The sacredness of law and justice, Exodus xviii.

13. The Jewish people to be "a peculiar treasure, a kingdom of priests, a holy nation" (Exod. ix. 16; 1 Peter ii. 5, 9); the bearing of this on the individual and social religion and morality of Christians.

14. The fundamental importance of every commandment in the Decalogue; affording abundant material for both simple and advanced teaching; Christ's "fulfilment" of the law.

15. The love of God; its meaning to the Jew; its fuller meaning to the Christian.

16. The significance of Pentecost to the Jew in Biblical and post-Biblical times; its further significance to the Christian.

17. The Day of Atonement; Jewish feeling about it in Mosaic and in later times; it suggests both simple and advanced teaching about repentance and the forgiveness of sins; early, prophetic, and Christian ideas about atonement, sacrifice, fasting, etc.

18. From the Law books it is possible to select many passages for teaching morality and social duties.

19. The book of Ruth; one of its lessons was a rebuke of Jewish exclusiveness.

20. The character of David; its mingled good

and evil; its idealisation by the later writers. In what higher sense was our Lord the "Son of David"?

21. The Psalms; a treasury of worship, thanksgiving, prayer, penitence, and all the deepest feelings of religion.[1]

22. Anthropomorphic ideas of God in the Psalms and other books. What moral and spiritual truths lie beneath them?

23. The historical books should be plentifully illustrated by selections from the Psalms and the Prophets.

24. Josiah's reform; the benefits resulting from it, especially the ultimate abolition of local sanctuaries.

25. The religious, political, social, moral teaching of the Prophets.[2]

26. The evidences of their special inspiration.[3]

27. Their doctrine of sin; how developed and modified by Christian teaching.

28. The nobility of Amos's teaching (chapter iii.): "You only have I chosen of all the families of the earth: *therefore* I will visit upon you all your iniquities"; the opposite and antidote to illiberal or Pharisaic patriotism, whether of nation, or public school, or social grade.

---

[1] Dean Church, *The Gifts of Civilisation* (Lecture on the Psalms); Professor A. F. Kirkpatrick (the Cambridge Bible).

[2] See F. D. Maurice, *Prophets and Kings of the Old Testament;* W. Robertson Smith, *The Prophets of Israel;* Dean Farrar, *The Minor Prophets;* Professor G. Adam Smith, *The Book of the XII.;* also Chapter IV. and the references given there.

[3] Professor W. Sanday, *Inspiration*, Lecture III.

29. Isaiah's teaching about Israel as the suffering "servant" of God; the meaning, use, and blessedness of suffering; the nobility and power of self-sacrifice (chapters xli., xlii.) fulfilled in Christ, and in all who live in the spirit of Christ. The reward of the servant's work, not anything selfish, but (as in St. Paul) the success of his work.

30. Jeremiah's "new covenant"; the fulfilment of his prophecy under the Gospel.

31. The religious and moral results of the Exile; the reformations under Ezra and Nehemiah incidentally show the great advance in the religion of the people since the age of Josiah.[1]

32. The growth of the doctrine (in Jeremiah and Ezekiel) that God's dealings and discipline affect not only nations, but also the souls of individual men.

33. Ezekiel's teaching about the shepherds and the watchmen applies to all who fill any post of trust or influence; the duty of moral courage.

Such suggestions are but gleanings from the rich field of religious, moral, practical teaching laid open to any one who enters devoutly and seriously on the study of the Old Testament; they are but scanty samples of the abundant harvest that may be gathered by the help of many writers who have laboured in this field of Biblical study.

But obviously many of these questions are

---

[1] Chapter III., *B*.

beyond the capacity of the average young girl or boy; they would therefore form no part of an elementary course. The elder pupils would, from effective teaching on such questions, gather ideas, impressions, influences, which would infuse into their Bible lessons the spirit of life. Nevertheless, the characteristic English reserve, shyness, inability to express ideas, and other hindrances, would prevent even elder pupils, certainly many of the boys, from adequately reproducing on paper the results even of the best teaching. Character and principle, piety, reverence, and the love of righteousness, may not be expressible in written answers, nor calculable in marks; and to persons who estimate the value of an educational subject by the number of marks that can be got by it, the best teaching might seem to be a comparative failure.

This being admitted, it still seems worth while seriously to consider whether writers of text-books, and examiners, might not do more to encourage teachers in giving great attention to the moral and religious truths of the Bible. In any case teachers, recognising that the examination test is both generally unavoidable and irremediably imperfect, will also recognise that their own teaching of the Bible is almost certainly inadequate if it can be adequately estimated by examination marks.

SCHEME OF SELECTIONS FROM THE OLD TESTAMENT

[The following is a tentative scheme of selections from the historical books of the Old Testament; it is framed on principles suggested in the preceding pages. In every case the selections include the last verse mentioned. A reference Bible (which is indispensable for teachers, and even for pupils) will show the connection of some of these passages with those in other books.]

GENESIS i.-iv.; vi. 5-ix. 19; xi. 1-9, 27-32; xii. 1-9; xiii.-xix. 28; xxi.-xxiv.; xxv. 19-xxxiii. 20; xxxv. 1-20; xxxvii.; xxxix. 1-xlvi. 7; xlvi. 28-end of book.

EXODUS i. 7-14; i. 22-vi. 13; vii.-xxiv.; xxxi. 18-xxxiv. 35; xl. 34-38.

LEVITICUS viii. 1-17; xxiii.-xxiv. 9; xxv.

NUMBERS x. 33-xi. 35; xiii. 17-xiv. 45; xvi.; xviii. 20-32; xx.-xxi. 9; xxii.-xxiv.; xxxii. 1-33.

DEUTERONOMY iv.-vi.; viii.; xii. 1-28; xvi.; xviii.; xxvi.; xxviii. 1-14; xxx.-xxxiv. 12.

JOSHUA i.; iii. 1-vi. 21; x. 1-14; xx.; xxiii.-xxiv. 33.

JUDGES ii.-iii. 7; iv.-vii. 25; xi.-xii. 7; xiii.

RUTH All.

1 SAMUEL	i.-iv. 22 ; vi.-xiii. 16 ; xv.-xxiv. 22 ; xxvi. ; xxviii. ; xxxi.
2 SAMUEL	i.-ii. 11 ; v. 1-12 ; vi.-vii. 29 (*cf.* 1 Chron. xxii., xxviii., xxix.) ; xi.-xii. 25 ; xv. ; xviii.-xix. 43 ; xxii.-xxiii. 7 ; xxiv. (*cf.* 1 Chron. xxi.).
1 KINGS	i. 5-iii. 28 ; iv. 20-vi. 1 ; vii. 51-x. 13 ; xi.-xiv. 31 (*cf.* 2 Chron. xii.) ; xvi. 29-xix. 21 ; xxi.-xxii. 40.
2 KINGS	ii. 1-22 ; iv.-v. 27 ; xvi. 1-20 (*cf.* 2 Chron. xxviii.) ; xvii.-xx. 21 (*cf.* 2 Chron. xxix.-xxxii.) ; xxii.-xxiii. 30 (*cf.* 2 Chron. xxxv.) ; xxiii. 31-xxv. 30.
EZRA	i. ; ii. 64-vii. 28 ; ix.-x. 17.
NEHEMIAH	i.-ii. 20 ; iv. ; v. ; viii. ; ix. ; xiii.

The prophetical books and the Psalms will be freely used for illustrations of the historical books. For this purpose a reference Bible will often be helpful ; but further guidance is needed by the aid of such books as are recommended in p. 58. The Rev. M. G. Glazebrook, in his *Lessons from the Old Testament*, gives a useful selection of passages.

The more important prophets will also be separately and specially studied in higher forms, for the reasons indicated in Chap. IV. p. 104 ff., and in Chap. VI. p. 166.

B.—THE INTER-TESTAMENTAL PERIOD

[The following short notes are meant simply to indicate the wide variety of interesting matter for lessons respecting this period; it is all helpful, and in part necessary, as a sequel to the Old Testament, and a preparation for the study of the New Testament. The section is an abridgment of notes for lessons given to a VIth form.]

It has been previously suggested that the purely political history of the Jewish nation should, for the sake of economising time, be disentangled from the history of the "Jewish Church": that is to say, the development of revelation, religion, and morality among the Jews should be traced without diverting attention to such political events as are less closely connected with this development. One of the sound reasons for such compression and abridgment of the Biblical narrative is that time may thus be gained for subjects to which too little attention has hitherto been given. For instance, it seems irrational, after following the history up to the time of Ezra and Nehemiah, to leave unnoticed a period of more than four centuries, during which the development of the Jews, and God's discipline of them, was not intermitted, and the preparation for the Gospel was further matured.

It is true that no canonical books of

Scripture shed light upon this interval, and that after Malachi (*circa* 432 B.C.) comes a period of some three centuries, of which scanty records are left in the history of Palestine. It is a period that shows some slight advance; the growth of a more catholic hope, and of a clearer belief in a future life; but more and more towards the close its history produces a sense of disappointment: "it is a trial to one's faith in the religious vocation of Israel; if the Divine spirit was immanent, whence came the sad decadence?"[1] Yet such periods of local ebb in the advancing tide of human progress are not unfamiliar in other historical epochs, for instance, in the age before the Reformation. The close of this period has been compared to the time in winter when seeds and kernels have grown dry and hard, and yet the promise of spring is at hand. The legalism of the Scribes and Pharisees served to bring into relief the inherent incompleteness of the law, and so prepared the way for Christ. And in spite of the discouraging semblance of failure, there were, between Malachi and the Advent, persons, events, movements of thought, changes of national character and feeling, which well merit more attention than they commonly

[1] Professor A. B. Bruce, *Apologetics*, p. 288 *sq.*

receive; not only because they present the natural sequel of the Old Testament history, but still more because they contribute much to the understanding of the state of Jewish religion and morality at the time of our Lord's coming. They enable us better to appreciate the reasons why, when "He came to His own, they that were His own received Him not"; and also how the seed-bed had been prepared for the fruitful sowing of the Word, first in the hearts of a faithful few; and then, after the Resurrection, widely throughout the Roman Empire.

Accordingly, it is suggested that material for some interesting and useful lessons to senior classes might be afforded by the following topics, for which details could be gathered from such books as *Josephus;* Stanley's *Jewish Church*, vol. iii.; Ewald, *History of Israel*, vols. v. and vi.; Edersheim, *Jesus, the Messiah*, vol. i.; the Rev. R. A. Redford, *Four Centuries of Silence; Judaea and her Rulers* (S.P.C.K.); Edersheim's *History of the Jewish Nation*, edited by the Rev. H. A. White; Mr. W. D. Morrison, *The Jews under Roman Rule;* the Rev. Arthur Carr, in the *Cambridge Companion to the Bible*, pp. 102-109; and, above all, E. Schürer, *History of the Jewish People in the*

Time of Jesus Christ (6 vols., T. Clark, Edinburgh, a mine of well-arranged information, with ample lists of books).

(*a*) The influence of the Exile and Captivity on Jewish religion and morality, producing a contempt and hatred of polytheism, and a final abandonment of it; and, as a natural result, a growing spirituality of religion and purification of morals.

Judaism could not have reached its higher developments without the exile to Babylon.[1] It taught the Jews a more catholic view of religion, that God's promises of mercy and grace were not limited to one spot on the earth, and that righteousness such as Daniel's was as possible in Babylon as in Jerusalem. It prepared the way for the final abolition of sacrifice; exiles debarred by the Deuteronomic law from sacrifices elsewhere than at Jerusalem had to learn perforce that it was possible to serve God without them. It paved the way for the belief and hope (expressed in the later chapters of Isaiah and elsewhere), that their religion would ultimately so develop and expand as to become no longer national but universal.

(*b*) The transference of the centre of gravity

[1] Mr. C. G. Montefiore, *The Bible for Home Reading*.

of Judaism to Alexandria, and the consequent fusion of Greek and Jewish elements of thought, learning, morality, and conduct among the Hellenists, whose greatest representative was Philo.[1]

(*c*) The LXX. version; its origin, character, importance; how it maintained the knowledge of the Law among the Jews of the dispersion, who were ignorant of Hebrew; and also was *ostium gentibus ad Christum*, spreading among the Gentiles a knowledge of the true God, and of His promises of a Messiah, which at the time of the Advent were current throughout the Eastern world. After the Ascension it was most helpful to the spread of the Gospel (*cf.* Acts viii. 28, xv. 21); those who were scattered abroad by persecution carried tidings of Christ, confirmed by the things written of Him in the LXX. Many of the Fathers used it; the old Latin version was a translation of it long used in the West, till superseded by Jerome's Vulgate, based on the Hebrew; it was translated into other languages, and, in fact, for a long period was the Old Testament of the larger part of the Christian Church.

The variations from the received Massoretic

[1] The Rev. T. B. Strong, *Christian Ethics*.

Hebrew text show that the LXX. editors used other, possibly older, MSS., which in some cases had better readings; and some of these variations appear in quotations from Old Testament in New Testament. A good example is found in Hebrews x. 5; and other very interesting instances are given by Robertson Smith from Jeremiah xxvii. 5 ff.,[1] and the narrative of David and Goliath in 1 Samuel.

Moreover, " the language of the LXX. is the mould in which the thoughts and expressions of apostles and evangelists are cast. It created a new religious phraseology, transferring Hebrew terms and ideas into a language teeming with ideas at variance with Hebraism,"[2] so that it is a treasury of illustration for the Greek Testament.

(*d*) The Apocrypha, which can now be studied with fresh profit in the Revised Version; in the *Cambridge Companion*, pp. 8, and 61 f., Professor Ryle gives a clear account of the several books, and of their relation to the Canonical books.

The LXX. version incorporated most of the Apocrypha, and many of the Fathers, know-

---

[1] *The Old Testament in the Jewish Church.*
[2] *Cambridge Companion to the Bible; Dictionary of the Bible*, article on the LXX.; Paterson Smyth, *Old Documents and New Bible.*

ing only Greek, accepted and quoted them as Scripture. The Western Church, using the old Latin version translated from the LXX., freely accepted them; and though Jerome excluded them from his revised Vulgate, they were subsequently added by others. At the Reformation, Luther and the other Reformers again set them apart; but the Council of Trent in 1547, by the vote of a small and illiterate majority, solemnly set them on the same level as the Canonical books, thereby lowering the standard which the Reformers jealously maintained. There is, indeed, a clear line of demarcation. The Apocryphal books are marked by their legendary and superstitious character, by their lower religious tone, and by elements of a new religious philosophy [1] due to Alexandrine influences. Some of these features obviously make them helpful to the system and traditions of the Romish Church.

It may be asked, how then are they profitable to members of Reformed churches? If once it is clearly understood that they are not applied to establish any doctrine, they serve "for example of life and instruction of manners." Moreover, they supply much

---

[1] The Rev. R. A. Redford, *Four Centuries of Silence*, chap. v.

material that is absolutely indispensable for the Church history of the four centuries between Malachi and John the Baptist; they show how God carried on the training of His people, in reverence for the law, in morality, in the growing belief of a future life and immortality; and they help to illustrate the New Testament by many coincidences of language and thought.[1]

(*e*) The cruel tyranny of Antiochus Epiphanes, and the wars of the Maccabees, afford striking examples of the good that may result from evil. From the time of Alexander, Hellenising influences became more and more powerful; in 175 B.C. they had already gained over the majority; and if things had gone smoothly, Judaism might either have been absorbed, or have become more eclectic even than the religious philosophy of Philo. The violence of Antiochus Epiphanes saved Judaism from this fate, and ultimately, in Palestine at least, Hellenism became entirely subordinate.[2]

(*f*) The wars of the Maccabees are interesting in themselves; and still more because they

---

[1] For an appreciation of their value in these respects, and also of their literary beauty and interest, see Dean Stanley, Lecture XLVII.; Dean Farrar on Wisdom, and Dr. G. Salmon's Introduction to the Apocrypha, in the *Speaker's Commentary*. [2] E. Schürer, vol. i. p. 194 *sqq.*

resulted in elevation and purification of the religious spirit, and in an ardent patriotism and national pride, which, in spite of adverse influences, survived to the Roman period as a living power; not the weakest among the national and popular sentiments that affected the ministry of our Lord, and the progress of the Church. Another outcome of this time was the growing strength of the belief in a future life and resurrection, which ultimately contributed to prepare men to welcome the preaching of " the kingdom of heaven."

(*g*) The establishment and growing influence of the synagogue system; its effect in promoting the growth of religious parties. The Pharisees were closely connected with the Scribes, who expounded the law. A singular fluidity, and want of system in religious belief, resulted from the Scribes' uncritical reverence for the very letter of the Scriptures, written in different ages, and far from uniform in their presentation of religious views. They ultimately "buried religion in the vast pyramid-tomb of the Talmud,"[1] and their system of teaching too frequently resulted in externalism, formalism, and inward scepticism.[2] Still

---

[1] W. S. Bruce, *Ethics of the Old Testament*, p. 241.
[2] Professor A. B. Bruce, *Apologetics*, p. 270; Mr. W. D. Morrison, chap. x.

the synagogue system was a means of maintaining personal devotion and piety, and thus it prepared the way for the time when the Temple, with its sacrifices and ritual, should disappear, and men should "worship the Father in spirit and in truth."

Moreover, all-embracing legalism fostered a high reverence for practical morality.[1] The sanctimonious Pharisees, whom our Lord so frequently condemned, were not the type, but the caricature of the normal Jew. "Rabbinic morality was simple and pure,[2] earnest yet cheerful, penetrating through Jewish society; men were fitted by it for the simple duties of everyday life, and also made ready for the sublimest self-sacrifice for the cause of God," such as was exemplified by the apostles and martyrs of the early church. In estimating the morality of the later Judaism a distinction must be drawn between the debased population of the capital, and the simple peasants of the country districts; just as imperial Rome, and modern Paris, cannot fairly be taken as representing the morality of the provincial districts.

Thus the Law, in more senses than one, was

---

[1] A. Edersheim, *Jewish Social Life*.
[2] Mr. C. G. Montefiore, *Hibbert Lectures*, p. 547.

a "schoolmaster to lead men to Christ," and some study of its continuous progressive influence on national and individual character during this period is helpful, if not necessary, for a just appreciation of that which helped, and that which hindered, the preaching of Christ's Gospel.

(*h*) The growing influence of Rome; at first favourable to Jewish independence by weakening the power of Syria; then after the Mithridatic wars becoming predominant in Judea; and later, in the times of Julius Caesar and Augustus, fostering the power of the Herods, whose public works, and especially the Temple, with its magnificent buildings and stately ritual, stimulated the patriotic and religious pride of the Jews and their jealousy of any rival system. On the other hand the Jewish settlement at Rome became later the seed-plot of the Roman Church, whose branches were to overshadow the world.

(*i*) An outline sketch of the condition of Jerusalem and Galilee at the time of our Lord's birth. Some such sketch is sometimes given as an introduction to text-books of the Gospel history. It would be useful to point out that Christianity, however much the law and other influences had prepared the way for it, was not a natural product of such antecedents; that the appearance of the Son of God, the "Son of Man," among such environments was not the result of ordinary historical evolution; but was in simple truth a miracle, analogous to that which followed the creative word, "Let there be light, and there was light" (*cf.* John i. 4, 5, 9).[1]

(*k*) In higher classes it might be well to speak of the preparation for Christianity during these centuries by God's providential guidance of the world's history, through (1) the spread of Greek influence, thought, and language; (2) the growing political influence and organisation of Rome. The pause in the development of Judaism is coincident with these successive or partly contemporaneous movements, originating in the conquests of Alexander and of Rome, like tide-waves flowing in from east and west. The results of conquests are not matured at once, and Judaism was to wait until the new forces and organisations had developed themselves. The Saviour was born when the fulness of the times had come through the convergence of

---

[1] Edersheim, *Jewish Social Life in the Time of Christ;* Professor A. B. Bruce, *The Miraculous Elements in the Gospels*, p. 334 *sq.;* Newman Smyth, *Old Faiths in New Lights;* Bishop Moorhouse, *The Teaching of Christ.*

the influences of Jerusalem and Alexandria, of Greece and Rome.[1]

C.—New Testament

The main object is to gather from the New Testament "that which is necessary to salvation" (Article VI.); and, for reasons previously given, this object should be pursued with as much directness as is possible, avoiding all that is relatively unimportant. Obviously the questions of primary importance are, "the steps of Christ's most holy life"; what He is; what He did and taught; what was His purpose in coming among men; how He effected it; in what ways He is an example to us; the significance of His death and resurrection; His foundation of a Church; its progress under the teaching of the Spirit. Parts of this scheme of instruction are plainly more suitable for senior classes; but in any case it is a full programme, demanding careful selection and arrangement of materials.

---

[1] For details see P. Schaff, *History of the Christian Church*, chap. i.; Archdeacon Cheetham, *Church History*, chap. i., and the authorities quoted by them; also the Bishop of Rochester's essay in *Lux Mundi;* Professor A. B. Bruce, *Apologetics*, Book II. (Internat. Theol. Library).

No one would propose to read the life of any great thinker, preacher, missionary, founder, in three or four differently arranged biographies, without any attempt to harmonise them, or draw the broad outlines of a consistent picture. But the life of our Lord is commonly studied by reading the three synoptic Gospels successively. Many of the discourses, parables, miracles, etc., are thus read repeatedly, sometimes in different order and combination, and with differing details. This causes not only an ill-arranged expenditure of time, but also confused notions of the relation and sequence of events. The result is that the history of our Lord's ministry, especially in Galilee, leaves in the minds of most boys and girls a very fragmentary and inconsequent idea of its progress and meaning. At a later stage of theological teaching it may become necessary to study carefully the distinctive features of the Gospels; but a clear view of the whole course and purport of the life of Christ should precede the examination of the characteristics of the writers of it.

Again, school programmes not uncommonly omit the whole or the larger part of St. John's Gospel. No doubt, the discourses, if studied in detail, are difficult for young people; yet even juniors should not be ignorant of

St. John's supplementary narratives respecting the ministry in Judaea; and the discourses, at least in outline, can be so explained to elder classes as to interest them deeply in the presentations of the Divine personality and higher teaching of Jesus. In fact, in the later stages of school life they are a necessary complement to the more rudimentary narratives of the synoptic Gospels. It is true that there is serious difference of opinion respecting the order of events in the Gospels. Still it is quite possible to agree upon a harmonic arrangement, after the manner of the old "Diatessaron," which, though not claiming to be scientifically accurate in its chronology and sequence of events, shall yet serve as a definite framework for the narrative.[1]

In this way the history of our Lord's life may conveniently be divided into lessons for three or four school terms, provided that attention be confined to such matters as shall help to produce a full, clear, living conception and picture of Jesus Christ, the Son of God, and His ministry. But some points that are now commonly insisted on may be reserved for

[1] Simple outlines of such a harmony will be found in Fuller's *Harmony of the Gospels*, S.P.C.K. (a translation of Tischendorf, used also in the Rev. A. E. Hillard's *Life of Christ*).

a later stage. Every one of the four Gospels is of inestimable value and interest; but some questions relating to their individual peculiarities, their relation to each other, etc., belong to the province of "higher criticism"; it is premature to introduce them into the teaching of younger pupils. It has been customary to get up lists of non-pertinent details, such as the parables or miracles peculiar to each gospel, and other special characteristics; but matters of this sort are far less important than that which is the central purpose of every one of the Gospels: they are written "that we may believe that Jesus is the Christ, the Son of God; and that believing we may have life in His name" (St. John xx. 31). Similarly, some of the helps to the study of the Bible, however well meant, may be practically hindrances to a living apprehension of its higher purposes, "tithing mint, anise, and cummin, and neglecting the weightier matters." A mass of detail diverts the attention, and confuses the picture; and young people may come away from lessons on the Gospels burdened with unimportant facts, yet without a clear and high conception of the person and work of Jesus; of the course, meaning, results of His ministry; of His methods of training His disciples for their future work;[1] of the gradual laying of the foundations of His Church and kingdom by influence, teaching, and ordinance; of the reasons and tokens of the growing hatred of His Pharisaic and priestly adversaries; of the different stages of the conflict in Galilee and Jerusalem; of His victory in spite of seeming failure.[2]

It should be obvious that even in junior classes the Gospel history should be immediately followed by some outlines of the history in the Acts, showing how the Lord's work was carried on by His disciples, and how His promises were fulfilled in the early history of the Church. In the senior classes, after a more detailed course in the Gospels, the Acts will in like manner be studied more fully, illustrated and supplemented by the correlated parts of the Epistles, so as to show the difficulties of various kinds that impeded the work of the Gospel; how they were overcome; the development of the Churches, and of Christian doctrine, under the influence of the Spirit; the traces of organisation in the infant Church.[3]

[1] Dr. H. Latham, *Pastor Pastorum*.
[2] Bishop of Durham, *St. John*; F. Godet, *St. John*; J. B. Mozley's University Sermon, *The Pharisees*.
[3] Such a study of the Acts has been rendered more

This scheme will once more require the compression or omission of some of the historical, geographical, political information that is commonly included in Divinity lessons on the Acts. About places of minor significance such details may be given sparingly, just enough to explain incidents in the narrative, and add some "local colour"; but they are sometimes allowed to overlay and obscure on pretence of illustrating. Similarly, the genealogy and family of the Herods, the personal history of Gallio, Felix, Festus, etc., are allowed to absorb needless attention. There are, however, some cities so closely concerned with the spread of Christianity that well-sifted information about them is almost essential; for instance, it is important to realise the shifting of the centre of gravity from Jerusalem to Antioch, and the part played by Ephesus.

It is even a question whether in higher classes it is well to devote to the Hellenistic Greek of the New Testament time that might

attractive, intelligent, and fruitful by the recent labours of Professor W. Ramsay. See *The Church in the Roman Empire* and *Paul the Traveller;* these books greatly strengthen the evidences of the historical genius of St. Luke, and of the genuineness and accuracy of his writings. See also the Preface to Blass's edition, and his article on the Acts in the new edition of the *Dictionary of the Bible.*

with greater advantage be employed on other subjects. It is, indeed, a convenient neutral ground, especially for those who know or like Greek better than Divinity; but the "ecbatic and telic" senses of ἵνα, or the peculiar uses of μή, may be made more prominent than some of the primary objects of the Acts and Epistles. It is desirable that candidates for Holy Orders should know much of Hellenistic Greek, and it is well that sixth-form boys should know something of it; but it is not so important to their religious education as school examination papers often seem to imply. On the other hand, more attention might well be given to the simpler parts, especially the ethical teaching, of the Epistles, without entering upon questions of " higher criticism." There are many chapters and passages which might be read even in junior classes; they would be compared with, and illustrated by, our Lord's teaching, so as to show how His apostles, guided by His Spirit, developed and applied what they had learned from Him. They would afford useful opportunities of inculcating the principles of Christian ethics, and serve as a substitute for, or an introduction to, a more formal treatment of this unduly neglected subject. Any teacher could easily select such passages. The following present themselves as the most obvious:—

> Epistle to Romans xii., xiii.
> 1 Corinthians xiii., xv.
> Galatians v. 16-vi. 10.
> Ephesians iv.-vi.
> Philippians iii.-iv. 9.
> Colossians iii.-iv. 6.
> 1 Thessalonians iv., v.
> 1 Timothy i.-ii. 7 ; vi.
> 2 Timothy i.-iii.
> Titus ii., iii.
> Philemon.
> Hebrews xii., xiii.

And selected passages from James, 1 Peter, and 1 John.

The whole of this list might be beyond the compass of a school programme, but it offers a rich field of choice for continuous or occasional lessons.

Note on the Influence of Examinations on the Teaching of the New Testament

I have read a large number of examination papers set to secondary schools of various grades by different examining bodies. They naturally vary in range and difficulty, but the character of them is singularly uniform.

There is a lack of discrimination between the facts that are and those that are not important, or rather a prevailing tendency to select those that are of the latter kind. Far too many questions are set on comparatively minute details, on places, persons, incidents that have little relation to the main purposes for which the Bible should be studied.

On the other hand, there is quite a singular want of such questions as encourage teachers and pupils to think of and enter into the moral and spiritual teaching of the inspired books. This defect is specially remarkable in papers on the Gospels. I have before me sets of papers composed for examinations affecting thousands of candidates in the years 1893 to 1895. In those three years successive papers were set on the three synoptic Gospels. They are such as to encourage or compel teachers to impart a knowledge of the special characteristics of the several books, and the additions, omissions, peculiarities in the narratives recorded by each; knowledge, no doubt, of much interest and value, but belonging properly to the department of literary criticism. Then there are questions on the Greek text, " explanations with reference to the context," meanings of parables, etc. etc. But a boy or girl who had passed through a three years' course on these three Gospels might have got full marks for these papers, and yet have no connected ideas about the personality of Jesus, the special character of His teaching, the purpose of His coming, the broad outlines of His life, etc.

No one would be content to read the life say of Luther, or Wesley, or Pitt, or Wellington, by such a method as these papers encourage. Even from a purely secular point of view such a method would be unintelligent. And it must be remembered that the influence of such papers on the teaching is resistless. No doubt many teachers look above and beyond the scope of the examination for which the pupils are being prepared; but a large majority will consider that their duty is fulfilled if, after studying the character and range of the examination, they have prepared their pupils to pass it successfully.

It may be said that these defects are inevitably inherent in any examination of such a subject as "Divinity"; or that criticism of existing papers and methods is valueless without some indication of a remedy. Some detailed suggestions are therefore offered (as in the case of the Old Testament) with reference to the kind of questions that may reasonably and profitably be included among the subjects of teaching, even in junior classes. Assuming that the life of Jesus Christ has been taught, or is being taught, with some attention to its historical course, much matter for teachers, perhaps even for examiners, might be found in the following topics. An apology for presenting such obvious suggestions in a manual for teachers may be found in the circumstances that tend to limit unduly the subject matter of average religious teaching.

1. The character of Jesus as the Son of Man; what is to be learned from His childhood and boyhood; His method of life, His voluntary poverty and suffering; how far they were helpful, or even essential, to His mission; His love, sympathy, compassion; His purity, humility, obedience; His manliness and courage; His freedom from passion, pride, ambition, love of popularity; His faith, devoutness, prayerfulness, knowledge of the Old Testament Scriptures; His freedom from prejudice; His discernment and dislike of hypocrisy; His liberality and catholicity; His claim of sinlessness, and all that this connotes; the miraculous combination of ap-

parently conflicting qualities; the manifold influence that such an "ensample" should have on those who claim to be His disciples.

2. Jesus as the Son of God; the marks of His Divinity in His history, words, and actions; His miraculous powers; the object of them; His self-restraint in the use of them; the light they throw on His nature, character, and mission; human acknowledgments of His Divinity, and His reception of them; the central importance of the Resurrection; "the teaching of the Forty Days."

3. Jesus as a Teacher: "He taught as one having authority, and not as the scribes"; the nature and explanation of the difference; His teachings about the Father, the Holy Spirit, the Christian Church, Baptism, the Lord's Supper, the Commandments, and their relation to Christian religion and morality; His teaching about the aims of life; about riches, almsgiving, thanksgiving, prayer, worship, faith, death, judgment, heaven, hell; the originality of His teaching; its relation to His "environment," and to previous teachers.

4. His relations to various sections of the Jews; His popularity with the common people; the causes of it, and His own action in face of it; why He was received in Galilee, rejected

at Jerusalem; the hostility of the Pharisees, Sadducees, and priests, and the causes of it.

5. Jesus as Prophet, Priest, King, Messiah; resemblances to, and differences from, the old types; in what sense "the testimony of Jesus is the spirit of prophecy"; Jewish misconceptions of His personality and mission; their causes and results.

6. Simple applications of the principles of the Gospel to modern life; their bearing on the aims of life, and the choice of a career; on self-denial, almsgiving, and the relief of the poor; on the duties of property, and the right use of "the blessings of this life"; on elementary social and civic duties.

Some of these questions may be mainly suitable for senior classes, but the large majority demand no more than knowledge of the facts about Jesus Christ and His teaching, coupled with elementary conceptions of their significance, in such a measure as is essential for intelligent understanding of what He was and what He came to do.[1]

[1] Books for reference are innumerable; among the more obvious are F. W. Robertson, *Sermons*; J. H. Newman, *Sermons*; H. P. Liddon, *Bampton Lectures;* Newman Smyth, *Old Faiths in New Lights;* Dr. A. M. Fairbairn, *Studies of the Life of Christ;* J. R. Seeley, *Ecce Homo*, especially chaps. xiv., xvii.-xxiii.; Bishop Moorhouse, *The Teaching of Christ;* Dr. H. Latham, *Pastor Pastorum*.

In answer to what has been said it might be urged that the Churches, by services, sermons, lectures, etc., provide supplementary instruction in the Christian Faith which may remedy deficiencies in school teaching. Such an answer might be valid in respect of the large number of elementary school children who attend Sunday schools in which systematic teaching is organised. But there are many pupils of secondary schools who have no similar advantages and opportunities, except in Confirmation classes (yet, as the time allotted to these does not usually exceed a few hours, it is not possible to cover the whole of the ground); or through such similar agencies as may exist among Nonconformists; and some few may be members of congregations in which the ancient and most wholesome observance of public catechising is maintained. The teaching of sermons and lectures is generally fragmentary and unsystematic; in most congregations it is addressed chiefly to adults, and it has to assume that the hearers already possess a framework of the essential truths and principles of the Gospel. If then such a framework is not built up by the teaching of the school, there is a probability that a large number of young people will grow up with most unformed conceptions of the elementary truths of Christianity.

Much that was said (Chap. I. p. 18, and Chap. III. p. 54) about the influence, and the corresponding duty, of examining bodies will apply *mutatis mutandis* to the subject now under consideration. To discover and apply a remedy for defects is, no doubt, more difficult. Sectarian divisions are wider and deeper in respect of the teaching of the New Testament; yet, after all, there appears to be no adequate reason against agreement about the right method of examining knowledge of the large body of fundamental Christian truth which is held in common by all, or nearly all, the Reformed churches. In any case examining bodies bear a responsibility proportioned to the influence they wield; and it is their duty to consider whether the present system of examinations is the best that is possible under existing circumstances; and if not, to improve it.

D.—Early Church History

There are strong reasons why this subject should be taught to elder pupils in outlines as far (say) as the end of the fourth century.

It is the natural sequel to our Lord's life, and to the Acts of the Apostles; and if judiciously presented in a form suitable to young minds, it is full of interest and instruction. To this end the teaching should be based on some such principles as the following :—

(1) The history should not be arranged on the annalistic plan, travelling steadily through the period in chronological order. Such a treatment is dry and confusing; the large, broad features of the Church's growth and progress are obscured by overlapping details.

(2) Heresies and strifes about doctrine should be kept as much as possible in the background; they are confusing and repellent to young people, who have as yet barely assimilated what is normal and catholic in doctrine. Besides, not a few heresies, even some which loom large in Church histories, were but of local or transitory importance; to make them prominent in early teaching is a mistake akin to that of giving undue prominence to irregularities in the teaching of grammar.

(3) The important topics, carefully selected

and limited, should be arranged under separate headings, as is done, for instance, in Archdeacon Cheetham's *Church History*, where the important facts are grouped so as to show [1] (*a*) the preparation of the world for the spread of Christianity; [2] (*b*) the outline of the struggle between the Church and the Empire; with special reference to Trajan, Hadrian, and Marcus Aurelius, and the reasons why persecution was inevitable, even under the best emperors; the main persecutions and their results; the ultimate victory of the Church and its causes. "The main cause of the ruin of the Empire was the moral deterioration of the lower classes; Christianity, if adopted in time, might have prevented this result." [3] (*c*) An outline of the attack and defence by argument, giving a brief notice of the principal assailants of Christianity and the apologists. If presented in a simple form, such an outline would show the moral and intellectual obstacles to the spread of Christianity, and the methods by

[1] For such outlines there is no lack of material in the Church histories of W. H. Simcox, J. C. Robertson, Archdeacon Cheetham, the Rev. A. H. Hore, and above all in Dr. Philip Schaff's *History of the Christian Church*, and the copious list of authorities cited by him.

[2] Bishop of Rochester's Essay in *Lux Mundi*.

[3] Bishop Westcott's "The Church and the World," in his *Epistles of St. John*; Professor W. Ramsay's *The Church and the Roman Empire*.

which they were overcome.¹ (*d*) The spread of the Gospel in the several provinces of the Roman Empire; the chief Churches and their characteristics; biographical outlines of a selected few of the chief representatives of the Churches (see § 4). (*e*) Very briefly, the development of catholic doctrine, with sparing references to the influence of Gnosticism, Arianism, etc.; the Apostolic and Nicene Creeds; not the Athanasian² (see § 2). (*f*) The organisation of the Church, which enabled it to withstand the opposition of the Empire, and ultimately to become its chief ally and support; with short details of worship, ceremonies, etc. (*g*) Christian social life and morality. With reference to this, Professor Sanday says,³ "The one thing that is most needed in the history of the Church, and of its institutions, is to ascertain truly and describe sympathetically, not the higher flights of genius within the Church, not the eccentricities of those who sought to recast Church life or Church doctrine, but the

---

[1] The translation of Justin's apology in Griffith and Farran's Library would supply matter for an interesting lesson to a senior class.

[2] Archdeacon Watkins' *Arianism*, chap. i.; Archdeacon Cheetham, §§ 96-102.

[3] *Guardian*, 23rd September 1896.

slow, steady, onward progress of the main body of mute inglorious Christians with those of their leaders, who are for us also mute and inglorious because they did not write, and have no historian." The difficulty of supplying such a demand is obvious; material may, however, be found in such early writings as the *Epistle to Diognetus*, the *Homilies* of Chrysostom, the letters of Pliny to Trajan; Aristides, *Apology*, 15-17; Eusebius, vii. 22; Tertullian, *Apology*, ix., xxviii.-xxxvi., xxxix., xlii.; *Ad Scap.* iv., v.; *De Spect.* i. See also Dr. C. Croslegh, *Christianity judged by its Fruits* (S.P.C.K.); Dr. C. G. A. Schmidt, *Social Results of Early Christianity;* Dr. P. Schaff, *History of the Church*, Part I. chap. viii.; Part II. chap. viii.; and the books referred to by him. C. L. Brace, *Gesta Christi*, chaps. i.-x., shows the influence of the Gospel during the Roman period on social and individual morality.

(4) The biographical element [1] (see 3) must be prominent. Young people ought to be made acquainted with the character and life-work of such men as Justin Martyr, Irenaeus, Clement of Alexandria, Origen, Tertullian,

[1] It is a question whether biographical notices should be inserted in their places in § 3, or grouped together in a separate section.

Cyprian, Eusebius of Caesarea, Athanasius, Chrysostom, Ambrose, Jerome, Augustine.[1]

If the foregoing principles are accepted as the basis of a Church history for schools, it will not be easy to find an existing text-book which satisfies the conditions. But if a demand arose for such a book it would no doubt be speedily supplied.

(The following words were spoken at the Head Masters' Conference, 1892, in reference to a resolution recommending instruction in Church history, passed at a Conference on Religious Teaching held at Sion College in June 1892):—

I entirely agree that Church history should be taught in all schools: in fact schoolmasters are doing that now; they are teaching the Bible history of the Jewish Church, and of the beginning of the Christian Church. If they are to add Church history of a later date, time must be found for it by economising in respect of the subjects that are already being taught. Now Bible history is not all Church history; much of it is the history of the Jewish people; similarly, English history is not entirely Church history. Jewish history, as a whole, is of course supremely interesting; yet there are parts of the general history of the

---

[1] Dean Farrar's *Lives of the Fathers*; Dr. A. Plummer, *The Church of the Early Fathers*; Dr. F. J. A. Hort, *The Ante-Nicene Fathers*.

Jewish people which are now of secondary importance to English boys, *e.g.* the details of the partition of the land of Canaan, the wars and conquests of Joshua and some of the kings, the complicated relations of the kings of Israel and Judah.

Economy of time in Old Testament teaching might be obtained by omitting or passing lightly over matters of secular history in order to find time for that which is closely related to the history of the Jewish Church; that is, to the system and discipline by which God prepared His chosen people to receive the Messiah, and to give their sons and daughters to be His followers, apostles, and evangelists.

Similarly, in teaching the New Testament, while teachers would not think of omitting any word of the Gospels or Acts, they would give less heed to more secular matters, such as the sites, history, and antiquities of Corinth, Ephesus, etc., in order that they might give more attention to the growth of the Christian Church, and the germs of the institutions and doctrines of Christianity and Christendom.

If later Church history is attempted, there must be a careful choice among the immense mass of materials. Church history is a part of *Welt-Geschichte*, world-history; it has to be studied in its relation to many secular political events; by itself it is comparatively unintelligible, at any rate after the first four centuries of our era. English schools usually do not attempt to teach world-history as it is taught in German schools; this is a reason why English schools might confine themselves to the history of religion in England. Again, the history of the Eastern and Western Churches is largely concerned with heresies, strifes, wars of religion, which are unedifying to the young. If, however, it is thought fit to teach general Church history, it should be in the spirit and on the lines of the admirable chapters in Guizot's *Civilisation in Europe*, in which he shows the influence of the Church in organising, moulding, civilising, and spiritualising the complex elements, first of the decaying Roman Empire, then of the feudal system and the growing nationalities of Europe.

Similarly in teaching English Church history much would be omitted that finds a place in the ordinary manuals. The object would be to show how, under God's providence, the English Church has been a main agency in civilising the country, and maintaining in it religion and piety. There would be a large use of biography; facts and principles would be grouped round the lives of such men as Bede, Theodore, Anselm, Langton, Wycliffe, Tyndale, Latimer, etc. It may be said that manuals for such teaching are not in existence, but if there were a call for them they would soon be produced.—[G. C. B.]

CHAPTER IV

THE INSPIRATION OF THE OLD TESTAMENT

"The word of God contained in the Old and New Testaments" may, to the most simple and ignorant believers, "become effectual unto salvation if they attend to it with diligence, preparation, and prayer, receive it with faith and love, lay it up in their hearts, and practise it in their lives."[1] But the study of the Bible raises in an educated mind questions of which one of the foremost is the inquiry into the nature, extent, and efficacy of its inspiration. No intelligent study of it is possible for him who starts with a false theory of inspiration resting on *a priori* notions of it; such theories have been, and still are, fatal obstacles to a just comprehension of God's ways of revealing Himself to man.

[1] The Scottish *Shorter Catechism*.

Inspiration is plainly asserted in Holy Scripture: "God spake unto the fathers through the prophets"; "The Holy Ghost spake through the prophets"; "The Spirit of Christ testified beforehand in them"; and it must be remembered that in the Jewish Canon "the Prophets" include the historical books.[1] But it is nowhere defined either in Scripture, or in the formularies of the Church (see Articles vi., vii.); its nature must be gathered simply from examination of the books themselves, and the method of their writers is clearly indicated by what St. Luke says of his own labours in compiling his Gospel[2] (Luke i. 1-3).

The leading characteristics of the books of the "Divine Library" may be briefly summarised as follows:—

I. Notwithstanding the very wide range and variety of these Scriptures, which embody traditions, documents, etc., of unknown antiquity, there is an unbroken but progressive unity of purpose; the revelations, and religious and moral principles contained in the earlier books, are on the same lines as those in the later, only less full, clear, and definite. No

---

[1] Professor A. F. Kirkpatrick, *The Divine Library*.
[2] Professor Driver, *Sermons on the Old Testament*, p. 146.

other literature is thus penetrated with a single purpose, and connected with a national history so unique in its character, progress, and results. It records the gradual training of the seed of Abraham, the chosen people, and the preparation for the coming of the Messiah from their stock. Successively or contemporaneously, the Law, the priestly sacrificial system, the monarchy, the prophets, the Captivity, the Return, and the "Interval," carry forward this education of Israel, and prepare the way for Him who fulfilled the Law; in whom, as Priest, King, Prophet, and suffering Redeemer, all the lines of this unique history marvellously converge, and find their complete synthesis and interpretation.

Attentive study of these facts confirms the belief, inherited by the Christian Church, that this unity is due to the influence of God's Holy Spirit, guiding not only the progress of the history, but also the writers whose records are our only witness to it.

II. Further examination shows (1) that this influence did not so act as to overcome the personality of the writers, or cause them to express themselves in the same manner. The writers made use of their ordinary human faculties in composing, compiling, editing, using existing materials and old traditions. They have recourse to different forms of literary composition, historical, poetical, dramatic.[1]

(2) The inspiring influence did not so work in them as to ensure accuracy in every minute detail of history. But such circumstantial errors lie within such narrow limits[2] as in no way to affect the general veracity of the record of facts, still less to impair the authority of the Bible in matters of faith and practice.[3]

(3) It acted on men who were in very different stages of moral development. God works slowly; it was no more a part of His plan to impart a completely developed morality in early times than it was to impart accurate scientific knowledge. Jesus speaks of a law of Moses in which a great moral principle was partly suspended; and the enactment was not intrinsically perfect, but was at that time adapted to "the hardness of their hearts." Training of any kind implies adaptation to imperfect conditions; and in this may be

---

[1] Mr. R. G. Moulton, *Literary Study of the Bible.*
[2] Professor W. Sanday, *Inspiration*, p. 161.
[3] Dr. C. A. Briggs, in *The Bible, The Church, and Reason*, chap. iv., quotes passages from Origen, Jerome, Augustine, Luther, Calvin, Baxter, etc., to confirm this qualifying view of inspiration.

found a solution of many of the common difficulties of Old Testament history, such as the sacrifice of Abraham, the deceitfulness of Jacob, the wars in Canaan, the patriotism of Jael, the imprecatory Psalms.[1] Professor Fairbairn speaks of "the intellectual innocence" of him who rejects the Bible because of its accounts of Cain, Jacob, David, etc. "If the Bible is absurd or ridiculous, the history of mankind, which has been so much influenced by it, is a march of unreason. The best progress of humanity has come from the Bible, and such innocent objections are based on a wrong conception of its nature."[2]

God did not make His people an entirely new creation under wholly new conditions; He took the sons of Abraham with their inherited characteristics and traditions; He progressively sifted out the evil and infused the good so as to produce something purer and higher than would have been developed without this special aid, guarding this product from contamination, and guiding its growth and expansion through all the vicissitudes of history.

It may be added that the moral difficulties of the Old Testament are complicated by

---

[1] Prof. Driver, *Sermons on the Old Testament*, pp. 149 ff.
[2] *Religion in History*, p. 104.

the practice, common in Hebrew writings, of ascribing men's purposes and actions to the direct intervention of God; and by a too literal acceptance of expressions such as "God spake," "The Lord said." Compare 2 Samuel xxiv. 1 with 1 Chronicles xxi. 1; the writers' different accounts of the origin of David's action indicate their meaning, and their estimate of his policy.

III. But it may now be asked, if all these qualifications are admitted, what then are the limits, the power, the value and authority of the inspiration of the Bible books? "The inspiration of the Old Testament is to be traced not so much in the form and matter of the records as in the moral and religious purposes that guide the writers. The fully developed 'Laws of Moses' appear to be the result of successive redactions and developments of traditions of a much older period. They derive their religious significance and value from the purpose that shines through them, and their relation to the pure religion that they helped to develop."[1] M. Lenormant (a Roman Catholic and a man of science) says: "L'inspiration Divine se trouve dans l'esprit absolument nouveau qui anime la narration."

[1] The Rev. W. F. Cobb, *Origines Judaicae.*

Inspiration has worked by a process of selection from materials of the most diverse kinds, on a system which progressively develops itself; so that while the Old Testament pays little attention to the course of material civilisation, it traces in preference the picture of moral progress and of religious truth. The exuberant polytheism of the Chaldaean histories has been eliminated to give place to the most severe monotheism; naturalist ideas of singular coarseness have been so modified as to express moral truths of the most spiritual order; and between the Bible and the sacred books most closely akin to them lies the interval of a complete revolution in human belief. The ideas become progressively more wide, pure, and spiritual from the early pages of Genesis to the call of Abraham, the promulgation of the Mosaic Law, and the mission of the prophets, who, in their turn, point onward to the supreme fulfilment in Jesus Christ and the kingdom of heaven.

If the very letter of the entire record is held to be inspired, experience has shown that new discoveries may at any time weaken belief in its value and power (though, in fact, recent discoveries have in many points brought fresh testimony to its accuracy);

but if the Old Testament is judged by comparing and correlating its moral, religious, and devotional purpose with that of the Christian system, the position is impregnable. "The Divine element in Scripture is indeed abundantly manifest; 'the heavenliness of the matter'—to use the expressive phrase of the Westminster Confession—speaks in it with a clearness that none can mistake."[1] The historians show how Israel was more and more separated from its neighbours to be a witness and keeper of the law of holiness and truth; in the Psalms[2] all the highest and deepest feelings of the religious soul are expressed, with a living power which makes them inexpressibly precious to the believing Christian; in the prophets shine forth sublime declarations of truth, righteousness, and judgment.

The function of the prophets was so important that it calls for somewhat fuller consideration.[3] The prophet differs from the ordinary teacher in that he produces something new.[4] Watching the stream of the people's life, he proclaims the advancing accomplishment of God's eternal counsels; in the present

---

[1] Professor Driver, *Sermons on the Old Testament*, p. 147.
[2] Dean Church, *The Gifts of Civilisation*, pp. 336 ff.
[3] See Chap. VI. p. 166.
[4] Dr. H. Martensen, *Christian Dogmatics*, p. 295 ff.

he shows at once the fulfilment of past types, and the visions of still more complete fulfilment in the future; for he recognises that the Old Covenant of Jehovah with His people is but preparatory for the New Covenant of a Messianic future. But in all his utterances he is but the channel of a Divine word "which was spoken by the Lord through the prophet" (Matt. i. 22), and this word is usually in close relation to contemporary history; the Divine Spirit who manifests Himself in the historical fact declares Himself also in the prophetic word which reveals the spiritual significance of the fact. Yet always prophecy, like knowledge, is "in part" (1 Cor. xiii. 9), fragmentary, limited by the mysterious relations of God's omniscient providence to the future of humanity, and to human freewill, until the fulness of time when type and prophecy were fulfilled and harmonised in Jesus Christ.

Messianic prophecy in its development through the centuries, from Genesis to Malachi, exhibits these positive and negative characteristics, and is the most convincing proof of Divine inspiration; not so much by the exact correspondence of prophecy with fulfilment, for "though there are undoubted examples of true prediction, yet the predictive element in the prophets is not so great as is sometimes supposed";[1] but rather by the marvellous convergence of apparently unconnected or incompatible types, features, foreshadowings, in the personality and life of Jesus of Nazareth.

But the prophets were far more than foretellers of the new covenant; they were God's chief instruments in the development and education of the chosen people, from whom the Son of David was to come forth.

Their predominant activity has given rise to the theory adopted by Renan and other scholars that the religion of Jehovah owes its birth to their "ardent meditations." Though such a theory cannot be reconciled with the facts of history and the ancient traditions of Israel, it may serve to throw into relief the strength of the prophetic influence through which, from the time of Abraham, Israel began and continued to be "the prophet among the nations," the chief depositary of the light of Divine revelation. It has been said that the strain of the prophetic teaching is an ever fresh variation on four main themes: what is not founded on righteousness must perish; Jehovah has revealed His righteousness to

---

[1] Professor Driver, *Sermons on the Old Testament*, p. 107.

Israel; Israel should fulfil righteousness; righteousness shall be fulfilled in the day of Jehovah.[1] Thus, proclaiming God's righteousness, protesting against evil without fear or favour, reminding the people of their duty to God, blending threats of God's judgments with most gracious promises of His favour, shedding on the darkest moments of national disaster the bright gleams of hope and future restoration, not only are the prophets of Israel unique among the writers of ancient times, but also their Divine inspiration is ratified and confirmed by the unique history of the chosen people. "The Old Testament does not simply contain prophecies—it is one vast prophecy; in the record of national fortunes, in the ordinances of a national law, in the expression of a national hope, Israel in its history, in its ritual, in its ideal, is, among the peoples of the world, a unique enigma, of which the Christ is the complete solution."[2]

The principles of selection and elimination, which are among the tokens of inspiration,

---

[1] James Darmesteter, *Les Prophètes d'Israel;* Professor A. B. Bruce, *Apologetics*, bk. ii.; Mr. C. G. Montefiore, *Hibbert Lectures.*

[2] Bishop of Durham, *Epistle to the Hebrews,* p. 491. (The whole excursus from which these words are taken is most valuable.)

can be effectively illustrated from the early chapters of Genesis. Taken in their literal simplicity, they have been a constant source of difficulties and a stumblingblock to believers; and have supplied materials for scoffing or serious objections, such as are absolutely unanswerable by the advocates of a verbal or mechanical inspiration in the present condition of science and literary criticism. Nevertheless in them, as in the higher parts of the Bible, there is an unfaltering testimony to God's holiness and His requirement of righteousness in man, combined with other marks of Divine guidance and inspiration.

(a) *The Creation.*[1]—Innumerable attempts have been made to co-ordinate a literal explanation of the Biblical narrative with the established facts of science; but in comparatively recent years archaeological discoveries have shown that the framework of the Scripture record is in all probability derived from an Assyrian tradition of great antiquity, which is also the original source of a Babylonian document, now in the British Museum, brought from the "library" of

---

[1] For the material for these paragraphs I am largely indebted to Professor Ryle's *Early Narratives of Genesis*.

Assurbanipal (who reigned 668-626 B.C.). In this instance the influence of inspiration is apparent in the purity and elevation of the conceptions of God, man, and the material universe. No similar influence can be traced in the early religious traditions of other nations akin to Israel, or indeed of any other nation known to history. They stand forth as revelations by the Spirit of God of some of the most vital and momentous truths of spiritual religion, communicated to Israel in ages when Egypt and other civilised nations of antiquity were groping in the darkness of polytheistic superstition. And these truths are set in a framework obviously intended as a help to the memory;[1] in fact, there is reason to consider it as a poem, but the poetry is so inspired as to be free from the tendency to deify the forces and phenomena of nature, and from other mythological superstitions of Chaldea, Egypt, and other nations of antiquity; it teaches that God by successive stages was the creator of matter, life, and human consciousness. Thus at the very beginning the history is based on principles of theology and morality which still under-

[1] Dr. Newman Smyth, *Old Faiths in New Lights*, chaps. iii., iv.

lie the religious creeds of the most highly cultivated nations of Christendom. God is set forth (not as evolved from chaos, or from pre-organised matter, not as one of a group of discordant deities, but) self-existing, the Maker and Ruler of all things, wise, beneficent, loving man, and hating sin. Man is presented (not as the degenerate outcome of some subordinate divinity, but) made in the image of God, deriving his life from the Divine Spirit, with a conscience, freedom of will, intellectual powers. The physical universe is (not essentially evil, or in conflict with the Deity, but) "very good" in His sight, brought into existence by His will, developed according to His plan, made subservient to the needs of human kind. "The Creator reveals His power as the power of wisdom and love by the production of a world endowed with freedom, and a limited measure of independent power."[1]

(b) *The Fall of Man.*—In this case also an ancient Semitic tradition appears to have been the common source both of the Bible narrative and of a corresponding Babylonian record. But Divine inspiration has infused such elements of purity and spirituality into the

[1] Dr. H. Martensen, *Christian Dogmatics*, p. 117.

old story that it has become the vehicle of new truths respecting freewill, temptation, sin, and retribution. Man is represented as free to choose between good and evil. The serpent (not to be identified with the later developed conception of Satan [1]) personifies the temptations of the lower desires and appetites. Man's choice to gratify them rather than obey the will of God brings upon him separation from God's presence, unhappiness, suffering, and death.[2] Yet God does not leave him without hope. Dimly and obscurely, after the manner of prophetic inspiration, yet in words that were full of growing significance to later generations, it is promised that "the seed of the woman shall bruise the serpent's head" (*cf.* Romans v. 12-21; xvi. 20).

An unexplained difficulty in the story, viz. the relation between sin and death, seems to

---

[1] See some interesting pages in Miss Julia Wedgwood, *The Moral Ideal*, 78-80, on the gradual development of the conception of Satan in the Bible, culminating in the book of Revelation; our Lord's words are very significant, Luke x. 18; Matthew xvi. 23; Matthew iv. 10.

[2] See an interesting passage on the Tree of Knowledge in Mr. C. G. Montefiore's *Bible for Home Reading*, p. 564. It has no parallel in similar stories of other races, though the Tree of Life is customary; the combination of good and evil indicates the relation of human wisdom and goodness to the knowledge of evil in its various forms of sorrow, suffering, pain, and sin.

be due to the tendency (visible through all the earlier periods of the Jewish history) to regard every form of material suffering as the direct punishment of evil-doing; and to an effort of the Biblical writer to suggest a solution of the insoluble mystery of the origin of evil. Speculations on this subject are frequent in Job, the Psalms, the Prophets, and the "Wisdom Books"; larger and more philosophical views were developed, and in the fulness of time the Cross of Christ shed some rays of light upon the mystery by showing the beauty and efficacy of "vicarious suffering." But in the main, the darkness is abiding; God, who permits many of His gracious purposes to be intelligible, has kept the veil over the origin of evil.[1]

The story of Cain and Abel, by its brevity, its omissions, its abrupt references to unexplained facts (such as the origin of sacrifice, the existence of blood avengers, etc.), indicates that here also earlier traditions have been sifted and compressed. But in this very short section Divine inspiration has once more communicated fresh spiritual truth; it has

[1] The symbolism of the Mosaic narrative of the Fall, the moral significance of the tree of life, the tree of knowledge with its tempting fruit, the serpent, is well explained in Martensen's *Christian Dogmatics* (translation, pp. 155-159).

shown self-will and rebellion against God leading to hardness of heart (Genesis iii. 9) and hatred against man;[1] God's warnings in the conscience (iii. 7); His anger against sin mingling with compassion and mercy (iii. 11, 15).

(c) *The Flood.*—Once more the narrative has affinities to a correlated "Chaldaean" record, preserved in a tablet of Assurbanipal's "library." The resemblances are as marked as the differences are significant. The Biblical writer represents the Flood as sent (not by the caprice of a junto of gods, but) by the one Almighty God as a punishment for sin; and then abated (not through the intercession of other gods, but) by the mercy of Him who sent it. The story shows also the value and power of faith (Heb. xi. 7), and the principle of the election and salvation of "a remnant," which is a distinctive feature of the theology of the Bible (*cf.* Isaiah vi. 13; x. 21; Romans ix. 27; xi. 4). In the theology of the later prophets, and of the New Testament, it becomes increasingly plain that the wise purpose and foreknowledge of God was designing, through this temporary method of election and particularism,

---

[1] *Cf.* 1 John iii. 12-15.

ultimately to benefit all the nations of the earth.

But, as before, the framework of the narrative displays the limited knowledge of the historian, and his adherence to details of the ancient story. Some terrible local visitation is conceived as affecting the whole of the known world; and the account of the creation (or appointment) of the rainbow as a token of God's covenant with man is a gracious relic of the ancient tradition.[1]

It may be remarked incidentally that this section supplies very clear and instructive evidences of the composite structure of the books of Scripture. In this case two documents, differing in style, phraseology, and incident, have been interwoven; yet so that their distinctive features enable scholars to disentangle and analyse them with a close approach to certainty.

These brief remarks may help to show by a few simple instances how a comparison of the Bible records with the corresponding religious traditions of other nations supplies evidence of the guiding and informing power of Divine

---

[1] For a good exposition of the Creation, the Fall, and the Flood on "traditional" lines see Edersheim's *Bible History*, vol. i. (R. T. Society).

inspiration in the Old Testament. But here and elsewhere the student of the Bible will always bear in mind that, as the revelation is progressive, there must be imperfections in the earlier stages (*cf.* the estimate of the Levitical system in the Epistle to the Hebrews). To use the Old Testament aright he must be filled with the spirit of the New Testament; for in this, as in every form of development, the final stage gives the standard by which the value of the earlier stages must be estimated. Such considerations are helpful, or even necessary, in face of difficulties that frequently occur in the study of the Old Testament, such as defective morality; crudity of the Law (Matt. v. 38, 39; xix. 8); exaggerated estimates of material prosperity; vindictiveness, as in some of the Psalms.[1]

[1] Professor A. B. Bruce, *Apologetics*, bk. ii. chap. x.

CHAPTER V

THE COMPOSITE CHARACTER OF THE BOOKS OF THE OLD TESTAMENT, ESPECIALLY THE HEXATEUCH

"HIGHER criticism" is so called to distinguish it from that which deals simply with the text of writings; its province is to discuss the integrity, authenticity, credibility, style, and other literary qualities of books. Its methods and tests, long used in the criticism of the classics, have now for many years been applied to the Bible; its results are variously estimated under the influence of cherished opinions and traditions.

But scholars of all schools have now come to a practically unanimous agreement that the five "books of Moses" and the book of Joshua (commonly grouped under the name of "the Hexateuch") were compiled from documents of different dates and of different authors. Dr.

C. A. Briggs gives a tabulated list, twelve pages long, of European and American scholars who hold what is called the "documentary" theory. He adds that those who have advocated in print the old traditional view "may be counted on one's fingers."[1]

The possibility of analysing the different elements in these and other parts of the Old Testament arises from the peculiar system on which Hebrew historical books are composed. In using older materials the historians do not rewrite the matter in their own language, as modern historians would do; they extract from the sources at their disposal such passages as are suitable for their purpose, and weave them together in such a way that the marked individualities of style and phraseology in the older writers are generally distinguishable in the compound result.[2]

Evidences of such a compound structure can be traced throughout the historical books, but nowhere more clearly than in the Hexateuch.

It may be convenient to give a brief summary of a theory respecting the structure of the Hexateuch which has obtained wide

[1] *The Bible, the Church, and Reason*, p. 122 ff.
[2] Bishop of Worcester, *Cambridge Companion to the Bible;* Professor Lias, *Principles of Biblical Criticism*, p. 132.

acceptance among students of the Bible. In the face of opposing arguments it cannot be taken as absolutely proved; but it has the characteristics of a good "working hypothesis"; it co-ordinates and accounts for a large proportion of the facts and features which have been disclosed by the scrutiny and analysis of many scholars. A full and clear statement of it is given in Professor Driver's *Introduction to the Literature of the Old Testament*. He, and those who agree with him, consider that the documents which have been combined in the Hexateuch are such as they are described in the following paragraphs.[1]

(a) The basis or framework of the whole is said to be a document distinguished by the name of the Priests' Code (indicated by the symbol P), because a large proportion of it, in Exodus, Leviticus, and Numbers especially, is devoted to details of ceremonial legislation. It aims at giving a systematic view, from a priestly standpoint, of the origin and chief institutions of the Jewish nation, with special attention to statistics and chronology. The prosaic and methodical style, and a multitude

---

[1] The Appendix to *Origines Judaicae* by the Rev. W. F. Cobb gives a convenient summary of arguments for the following analysis.

of peculiar words and phrases, mark it off from the other constituents that are woven together with it. By the majority of critics it is considered that this is the latest in date of the elements of the Hexateuch, belonging approximately to the period of the Babylonish captivity subsequent to Ezekiel, and being a codification of various ceremonial laws and regulations that had been developed from the time of Moses.

But there is much difference of opinion as to the dates of the origin and enactment of the several laws and institutions which the priestly writer thus compacted into his definite framework. Moses was undoubtedly the founder of the national and religious life of Israel. The nucleus of his teaching is preserved in the Decalogue and the " Book of Covenants " (Exodus xx.-xxiii.), and for the rest the most tenable account is that the chief ceremonial institutions are of very ancient origin; but the laws and regulations respecting them were gradually reshaped and developed, and the " Priests' Code " represents the form which they finally assumed. Its sacrificial and ceremonial enactments are contained in Exodus xxv.-xxxi., xxxv.-xl.; Leviticus i.-xvi., xxvii.; Numbers i.-x., xv., xviii., xix., xxv. 10-xxxvi.[1]

[1] Professor S. R. Driver, *Deuteronomy*.

Further, in Leviticus xvii.-xxvi. is a group of chapters which appear to be an independent and probably older code, now incorporated in the priestly code. The duty of holiness is here insisted upon with special emphasis and frequency, and this section has consequently been marked by the title of "the Law of Holiness"[1] (indicated by the symbol H).

(*b*) An early narrative, usually designated as JE, because it is itself compiled from two earlier writings, which use respectively Jehovah and Elohim as the name of God. The characteristics make it probable that J was written in the southern, E in the northern kingdom; they give prominence in their history to Judah and Ephraim respectively. The date of them is most probably not later than the earliest of the canonical prophets, *i.e. circa* 750 B.C.; in all probability it is decidedly earlier, written possibly in the earlier centuries of the monarchy, but incorporating

---

[1] On the antiquity of much of the ritual and sacrificial system thus formulated see the Rev. T. B. Strong's *Christian Ethics*, p. 41 ff. "The ritual enactments are in very many cases archaic in type, characteristic of an extremely early period of religion. Professor Robertson Smith has shown that the Levitical sacrifices are based upon ancient conceptions traceable throughout early Semitic history, and though later ideas are grafted on to the old system, the basis of it is antecedent to our earliest history of the Jewish people." *Cf.* Robertson Smith, *Religion of the Semites.*

much older material. It is not, however, archaic in style, but "belongs to the golden period of Hebrew literature." From its tone and other distinctive features JE is sometimes called the "prophetical narrative."

It includes a simple primary code of religious and civil law in Exodus xx.-xxiii., xxxiv. 10-26, xiii. 3-16.[1]

(c) The book of Deuteronomy.[2] It is argued that this was composed before P and JE had been combined, because the differences of detail between Deuteronomy and P are in many points only to be explained by the supposition that the two systems of law represent the usage of two distinct periods of the nation's life. Also it must be considerably later than JE, for its laws imply a higher civil organisation. The actual date of it cannot, however, be later than 621 B.C.; and there is high probability that it is "the book of the law" presented in that year to King Josiah (2 Kings xxii. 8 ff.); the reformation carried out by him was certainly on the lines of Deuteronomy. Its legislation is based mainly on JE, and in some cases is parallel

---

[1] For details of the passages included in JE see Professor Driver's *Introduction*.
[2] Professor S. R. Driver, *Deuteronomy*.

with H. In the latter case the materials are apparently derived from a common source; but it displays irreconcilable divergences from P, though at times alluding to laws similar to those in P.

The book is unique among the writings of the Old Testament by its strong individuality, oratorical power, and warm and persuasive eloquence. "Nowhere else in the Old Testament is displayed such generous devotion to God, such large-hearted benevolence towards man; nowhere are duties and motives set forth with such depth and tenderness of feeling, elevating the life of the community by the power of high principles. Its style, smooth, copious, impassioned, distinguishes its literary form from that of any formal official code; it was a prophetic formulation of the law of Moses adapted to the requirements of that later time; in it God's wisdom made provision for the spiritual survival of His chosen people on the eve of their political annihilation."[1] The influence of Deuteronomy upon the subsequent books of the Old Testament is clearly traceable in the historical books, and in the writings of Jeremiah, Ezekiel,

---

[1] Professor S. R. Driver, *Deuteronomy*, Introduction; Professor H. E. Ryle, *The Canon of the Old Testament*.

and the latter part of Isaiah; and our Lord Jesus set his seal on the value of this prophetic book by his quotations from it on the occasion of His Temptation (Deuteronomy vi. 13, 16; viii. 3). Its religious value is very great; it teaches that religion is not concerned merely with the intellect and the will, but with the exercise and right direction of the affections; it makes religion the real basis of all moral and social order, transfers it from national observance to personal consciousness, and thus aims at regenerating the community by the love and loyalty of individual souls; in fact, its teaching points directly to the kingdom of heaven to be founded by Christ.

In this case again there is great division of opinion as to the date and authorship. It does not actually claim to be written by Moses, but it represents Moses as speaking in his own person, issuing commands, and enacting laws as God's representative to Israel. How far, then, is the form of it consistent on the one hand with historical truth, on the other with the statements just made respecting the date and contents of the book?

An effective answer is given to this question by a writer who is allowed to be a good representative of the moderate conservative school of Biblical criticism, and who, as Professor of Oriental Languages at Glasgow, speaks with authority on the question under discussion.[1] He draws attention to the peculiarity of the Hebrew language, that it has not developed what we call "indirect speech"; it always gives, or professes to give, the actual words spoken; and from the beginning to the end of the Old Testament it remains always at this stage. Moreover, it was quite consonant to the spirit of Hebrew literature that a writer at a later date, whether soon or long after Moses (recalling the events of national history, and using we know not what documents; seeing the actual development of events which were only in germ in Moses' time, and the changes and modifications of Mosaic laws under the influence of past circumstances), should adapt the Mosaic traditions to the time at which he wrote, not inventing history or law, but setting forth in Moses' name that which had become under Divine guidance the outcome of Mosaic laws and institutions. Thus the book is "a revised and enlarged edition of the Book of the Covenant," a prophetical law-book, owing

[1] Professor James Robertson, *Early Religion of Israel.* Cf. *Church Quarterly Review*, October 1892.

much to the teaching of Hosea, and also of Amos, Micah, and Isaiah.[1]

On the other hand, the advocates of the traditional view repudiate this "dramatic" interpretation, and consider that it would have been simply dishonest to put into the mouth of Moses a series of discourses of such a nature. One of their main arguments (developed fully and ably by Bishop Ellicott in his *Christus Comprobator*) is that opinions on the authorship of the "Books of Moses," and of other books of the Old Testament, must be strictly governed by what our Lord said about them. If in quoting a passage He assigned it to Moses or David, there can be no further discussion; *e.g.* Mark x. 3 and Deuteronomy xxiv. 1; John v. 46 and Deuteronomy xviii. 15, 18; Matthew xxii. 44 and Psalm cx. 1.

They entirely decline to accept any of the arguments urged to reconcile our Lord's method of quotation with the results of criticism; viz. (*a*) that it was no more part of our Lord's mission to teach Biblical criticism than to teach natural science, and therefore His references to Scripture are adapted to the opinions

---

[1] On the other side see Professor Stanley Leathes, *The Law in the Prophets*.

current among His hearers; (*b*) that if He had attempted to traverse received ideas about the Scriptures, He would have raised difficulties, perplexities, animosities which would have seriously and needlessly aggravated the hindrances to His work; (*c*) (a more doubtful and hazardous argument, concerned with matters which lie "beyond the veil"), that our Lord, in taking our nature upon Him, had for the time "emptied himself" (Philip. ii. 6, 7) of some of the attributes of the Deity, and that His knowledge in this matter, as in another (St. Mark xiii. 32), was subject to limitations.[1]

Those who decline to accept any such explanation of our Lord's method of quoting the Old Testament Scriptures have yet to find an adequate answer to the difficulties arising from a study of the historical books; such as what Bishop Ellicott[2] calls the "apparent fact" that the historical books indicate that the Mosaic law was not observed, even in its most stringent ordinances, between the entry into Canaan and the times of the early kings. One answer suggested is that the ordinances

---

[1] Canon Gore's *Dissertations;* Bishop Moorhouse, *The Teaching of Christ,* p. 25 ff.; Luke ii. 52.
[2] *Christus Comprobator,* p. 73 ff.

in Deuteronomy and the Priests' Code were prophetic, pointing forward to a time when they could be complied with. Another writer says: "Our theory is that both JE and Deuteronomy are founded on traditions current in Moses' time, and on writings to be traced (though we may not be able to trace them) to Moses himself."[1]

The foregoing analysis of the Hexateuch, and the facts and arguments by which it is corroborated, appear to indicate a *via media* between the less convincing explanations offered by defenders of the "traditional" views,[2] and the wild, unhistorical theories of the extreme school of critics, which are repudiated by the learning and judgment of the best English theologians.

An example of the dangerous extravagance of such theories is quoted by Professor J. Robertson in his *History of Israel*, p. 469, from Maurice Vernes (*Résultats de l'exégèse Biblique*), who says: "The theologians and writers of the post-Exile period have been able to give such a life-like character to their

[1] *Church Quarterly Review*, January 1896.
[2] For a statement of these views, and arguments against the foregoing analysis, see Professor Lias, *Principles of Biblical Criticism*; *Lex Mosaica*, a series of essays by different writers, edited by the Rev. R. V. French; Professor Stanley Leathes, *The Law in the Prophets*.

creations that posterity has been thereby deceived, and has believed in a Moses living 1500 years before our era; whereas this Moses was only created in the fourth century." This extract illustrates the serious importance of care and discrimination in the selection of books on this difficult subject, lest teachers and pupils should be led astray by speculations unsupported by facts.

CHAPTER VI

CHRISTIAN EVIDENCES

[Some reasons for including this subject in the school course of elder pupils may be gathered from the arguments of Chaps. I. and II. See also the Rev. C. W. Formby, *Education and Modern Secularism*.]

AT the outset it is well to recognise what is the real value of studying a scheme of Christian evidences. It can do comparatively little for the conversion of unbelievers; men are not argued into faith, which lives far more in the heart than in the reason.[1]

But it can do something to safeguard, confirm, and develop faith, especially in the rudimentary stage, by showing that the reasons for it are manifold and convergent; by anticipating common objections and difficulties, and showing that they are either groundless, or far less formidable than they at first

---
[1] Pascal, *Pensées*.

appear to be; and by helping to dispel the notion, very prevalent in our day (and not uncommon in the past), that Christian faith is no longer tenable, because there are more rational explanations of the facts of human life. For it can be shown that far greater difficulties have to be faced by every other system of religion or philosophy which fairly attempts to embrace the results of history and experience, and to frame an hypothesis that shall cover the sum total of human life.

The following pages are based on notes of lectures delivered to a sixth form in 1891 and 1893. After careful inquiry it appeared that no suitable text-book exists, and the notes were compiled from a number of books, mostly easy of access, to which frequent references are made. The results of the teaching were tested by an independent examiner, and appeared to show that the subject had interested the boys, and that the method of treating it had been intelligible. These preliminary remarks may obviate the idea that such a course is too complicated and difficult for class teaching, and also may serve as an excuse for the brief disjointed form in which the facts and arguments are presented. The object is to offer a kind of syllabus, which may be easily expanded by help of the books that are quoted or referred to. To develop it in a literary form would require far more space than can be allotted to the subject in this elementary book.

Introductory

Some of the chief possible theories about God, the world, and human life:—

1. *Atheism.*
2. *Agnosticism.*—Based on an illogical confusion of the relations and provinces of knowledge and faith; or (in its commoner and more prevalent form) on an absence of, or indifference to, knowledge or inquiry about the facts and arguments which support faith.[1]
3. *Deism.*—Belief in a personal God who acts only through the laws of nature; prevalent in England in the latter part of the seventeenth century and the earlier part of the eighteenth.
4. *Theism.*—A much wider term, including most forms of monotheism, *e.g.* the religion of Israel, Mohammedanism, and modern theories, such as Unitarianism.[2]

[1] See p. 177.
[2] Professor Robert Flint, *Theism;* and article on Theism in *Encycl. Britt.*

5. *Polytheism.*

6. *Pantheism.*—Belief in a Divine power, not personal, but infused into nature, and finding its expression in the products and energies of natural forces.

7. *Positivism.*—In its best-known form, a singular modification of utilitarian philosophy, in which the conception of God is superseded by the abstract idea of Humanity, past, present, and to come, to which every individual of human kind owes service, allegiance, and even worship.

It is presumed that for the great majority of pupils in secondary schools, discussions about the being and nature of God are not necessary; and that the teacher may begin by assuming that which is the foundation of the religion both of the Old and New Testament: belief in a personal God, whose attributes are holiness, righteousness, wisdom, and love.

He may assume also the probability that such a God will make Himself known to such of His creatures as are capable of knowing Him, and this not merely by the facts and "laws" of nature, but also by some direct revelation.[1]

---

[1] Inverted commas are meant to indicate that "laws" of nature have no connection with legislation of any kind;

Facts and "laws" of nature are the subject of knowledge; the revelation of an infinite God to finite man cannot be the subject of knowledge in the same sense and degree; knowledge must be supplemented, in some matters replaced, by faith in that which is and must be unseen.

Faith in its most general form is clearly defined by Bishop Pearson, *The Creed*, vol. i. p. 4 (1847); its essence is assent to adequate testimony; the testimony may be so strong that faith may ultimately grow into a kind of knowledge (*cf.* John vii. 17). The nature of faith is illustrated by the fact that in the Old Testament the word is hardly found at all; it is replaced by "trust." But the Christian faith does not rest simply on presumptions, probabilities, or trust in God's goodness and veracity; it has also historical foundations.[1] The most important of these is laid in the doctrine of the Resurrection of Jesus Christ; this, then, may be first considered as an evidence of the Christian faith.

much confused reasoning may be confuted by pointing out the essential difference.

[1] Bishop Goodwin, *The Foundations of the Creed*, p. 441 ff.

A.—The Resurrection, a Historical Fact; the Testimony of the Apostles to it as the Keystone of the Faith

I. Of the written testimonies the earliest in date is that of St. Paul, especially in his 1st Epistle to Corinthians, written in 57 A.D., less than thirty years after the Resurrection (as though a man, now in mature life, were writing of what happened in his own country since 1867). It should be added that this is one of the Epistles whose authority and authenticity is now undisputed. In chapter xv. 3-11 are included six separate testimonies of Jesus's appearances [1] after His crucifixion, to—

> (1) St. Peter; nowhere described in the Gospels, but referred to in St. Luke xxiv. 34.
> (2) The Twelve (*cf.* Matt. xxviii. 17).
> (3) "Five hundred brethren at once, of whom the greater part remain unto this present."
> (4) St. James; not recorded elsewhere, but

---

[1] Bishop Goodwin, *The Creed*, p. 201 ff. ; F. Godet, *Defence of the Christian Faith*, pp. 1-53; Professor W. Milligan, *The Resurrection of our Lord.*

St. Paul knew him personally (Gal. i. 19 ; ii. 9).

(5) " All the Apostles " (*cf.* Luke xxiv. 50-53 ; the leave-taking before the Ascension).

(6) St. Paul himself. The line of argument in 1 Cor. xv. plainly shows that he is referring not to a vision, but to a bodily appearance of Jesus; he was absolutely convinced of the fact, and his life and labours are the proof of his conviction.

II. The Gospels. The first three, in their present form, incorporate traditions and writings of a much earlier date.

(*a*) St. Matthew—
  (1) To the women, xxviii. 1 ff.
  (2) To the Eleven in Galilee, xxviii. 17 (*cf.* § I. 3).

(*b*) St. Mark—
  (1) To Mary Magdalene, xvi. 9.
  (2) To the two going "into the country," xvi. 12 (*cf.* St. Luke xxiv.)
  (3) To the Eleven, xvi. 14.

[It should be added that there is doubt about the authenticity of Mark xvi. 9-20 as a part of the original Gospel. The passage appears, however, to be "older than the time when the Canonical Gospels were generally received; it is doubtless founded on some tradition of the apostolic age."[1]]

(c) St. Luke—
    (1) To two going to Emmaus, xxiv. 13 ff.
    (2) To St. Peter (*cf.* § I. 1), xxiv. 34.
    (3) To the Eleven (*cf.* § I. 2), xxiv. 36.
    (4) To the Eleven (*cf.* § I. 5), xxiv. 50.

(d) St. John—
    (1) To Mary Magdalene, xx. 1 (*cf.* Mark xvi. 9).
    (2) To the Apostles without Thomas, xx. 19.
    (3) To the Apostles with Thomas, xx. 26.
    (4) To seven disciples at the Lake of Galilee, xxi. 1.

Fully to estimate the value of these converging testimonies in the four Gospels it would be necessary to discuss the relations of the several Gospels to the others, a question too large and complex for the present purpose. It may be sufficient to point out that the independence of the testimonies is indicated by the variation of detail, their veracity by

---

[1] Westcott and Hort's Greek Testament, vol. ii. p. 28 ff.

the agreement in substance; they combine into a consistent picture.¹

III. St. Peter—
 (1) Acts ii. 32.
 (2) 1 Peter i. 3.

Another very strong evidence of the truth of the Resurrection is the immediate effect that the belief in it produced on the character and actions of the apostles.²

The witness of the apostles to the Resurrection was their primary duty (Luke xxiv. 48; John xv. 27; Acts i. 8, 22; ii. 32), and the effect of it was immediate and widespread. It is admitted by Strauss, Baur, and other negative critics that this testimony was not a fraudulent imposture, but based on honest belief; and they cannot deny that on their belief in this historical fact is based the historical development of the Christian Church, which thus becomes an auxiliary evidence of great and increasing weight.

But may they not have been honestly mistaken? Instead of an actual resurrection from the dead may there not have been simply a revival from a swoon or lethargy?

---

[1] Goodwin, p. 203; Godet, p. 16.
[2] Professor Milligan, p. 46.

Full discussion of this suggestion has shown that the objections to it are unanswerable, and that it must be abandoned.

The only remaining hypothesis (still seriously maintained) is that Jesus's supposed appearances were but visions and hallucinations arising in excited imaginations. But the witnesses testify that they heard discourses and touched Jesus, that He ate and drank with them. Hallucinations are marks of a morbid constitution of mind, yet the acts and writings of St. Peter and St. Paul show their perfect sanity and good sense. And is it possible that 500 people assembled together could persuade themselves that they saw the same vision simultaneously? Again, hallucinations are the reflections of excited hopes and expectations. But after the crucifixion Mary Magdalene, the women, the apostles, the disciples at Emmaus, show no signs of hope; believing Jesus to be dead, they are utterly dispirited. Finally, if Jesus, having died, did not revive, what became of His body? The answer to this question is more difficult than it seems at first sight.[1]

---

[1] See Dr. G. P. Fisher, *The Grounds of Theistic and Christian Belief*, pp. 170-174; he quotes Keim's conclusion that the hallucination theory is untenable.

This body of testimony establishes the Resurrection as a historical fact, of which the evidence cannot be explained away by those who refuse to accept its historical truth. This truth receives additional support from the following considerations of the importance of the doctrine of the Resurrection as a keystone of Christianity, and indeed of God's revelation of Himself to man: (1) its satisfaction of the widespread hopes and beliefs of mankind in many ages and countries; (2) the victory which the Church achieved by the preaching of the Resurrection; (3) the abiding and growing influence that it has exercised over the character and destiny of mankind.[1]

B.—Miracles

The Resurrection is closely connected with the Incarnation and the Ascension. Assuming that God wills and desires to reveal Himself to man, the *a priori* reasonableness of the great central doctrine of the Incarnation rests on strong argument. Yet, ultimately, it is a matter of faith resting on the testimony of St. Matthew (who is supposed to have gathered the facts from Joseph), and

---

[1] Goodwin, p. 217.

still more of St. Luke (who may well have derived it from the mother of Jesus); and there is much to prove that St. Luke was a singularly careful and accurate witness.[1] Further support to this doctrine is given by evidences to be adduced later.

All these great events are miraculous. They are, therefore, disbelieved by those who say (not that miracles are impossible, this is now admitted to be an unscientific statement, but) that "they never happen." Of course if this statement is accepted as axiomatic, argument and evidence become useless. But what right has it to be considered an axiom? A more scientific course is to consider the credibility of miracles in general, and then the arguments in support of particular miracles of cardinal importance.

I. The credibility of miracles in general, or of what is sometimes called "the supernatural;"[2] (a question-begging expression on which many unsound arguments have been based). It is said "miracles never happen"; but one miracle,

---

[1] Professor W. Ramsay, *The Church and the Empire;* and *St. Paul the Traveller.*

[2] J. B. Mozley, *Miracles;* Archbishop Trench, *Miracles* (introductory chapter) ; G. Warington, *Can We believe in Miracles?* (S.P.C.K.) ; Professor A. B. Bruce, *The Miraculous Elements in the Gospels.*

the Resurrection, cannot be explained away; no tenable theory has yet destroyed its historical basis. This fact shakes the presumption against miracles, so far as it rests upon the absolute uniformity of the "laws" of nature. Yet experience appears to prove this uniformity. How then can experience be reconciled with miracle? One answer is that for adequate moral reasons God may supersede the action of His ordinary "laws" of nature by higher "laws" as yet unknown to ordinary experience. This argument may be illustrated by the progress of science, which has shown both how much and how little any given generation may know about the possibilities of the "laws" and forces of nature. Conceive Hume or Franklin told about telephoning from London to Paris, or hearing a poet's or statesman's voice after his death. According to this line of argument what is called the "supernatural" may be simply a higher unrevealed form of the "natural," *i.e.* there is no difference of *kind* between ordinary events and miracles.[1]

This argument may be confirmed by the

---

[1] See Aubrey Moore, *Science and the Faith*, p. 104; and *Appendix,* p. 225; also Archbishop Trench on *Miracles*, chap. ii.

analogy of the action of man's will, when, for his own purposes, he supersedes or interferes with physical "laws" and forces by introducing others: *e.g.* a chemist, or a man throwing up a stone. Thus while "nature conceals God, man reveals Him" by the action of a will and personality derived from, and having analogies with, the Will and Personality of God.[1]

Moreover, in the history of the Universe there are periods of "Divine initiative," or new beginnings; at the creation of matter; at the introduction of the germs of life; at the commencement of self-consciousness in man; each of these has been a departure from the preceding uniformity of Nature, analogous to a miracle.[2]

The credibility of miracles is much supported by arguments which show the need of them as:

(1) Attestations of a revelation, vouching for the reality of it. Supposing, for instance, that Jesus had spoken all His discourses without working any miracle, what would have differentiated Him *in kind* from Socrates or Confucius? Would His hearers have had adequate evidence of His Divine mission?

---

[1] Dean Mansel in *Aids to Faith* (1861).
[2] Goodwin, p. 138.

Cf. John v. 36, "The works that I do, bear witness of me, that the Father hath sent me"; xiv. 11, "Believe me for the very works' sake"; x. 38; xv. 24. If it be answered that Mohammed succeeded without miracles, the answer is that his success was largely due to the use of means which Jesus deliberately rejected.

It may, in fact, be argued that miracle, especially "physical" miracle, is necessary as an instrument, or as a guarantee, of communications between the invisible and the visible order of things, when there is an adequate object for such communications.

Miracles attested the revelations made by Christ and His apostles; from their doctrine resulted the regeneration of mankind. Such a result was an adequate end for Divine intervention by miracles; when this object was so far accomplished that new agencies had been set at work for carrying it on, miraculous agency ceased to be necessary.

(2) Miracles are often "signs" of moral and spiritual truths, the seal of a Divine teaching which cannot be dissociated from them, and which in its turn becomes a main guarantee for the reality of them.[1] "The

---

[1] Godet, p. 149.

miracle seals the doctrine, the doctrine tries or tests the miracle." This argument applies again most obviously to "physical" miracles, such as Jesus's works of healing. "Moral" miracles, which are of a higher order, such as the character and teaching of Jesus,[1] confirm and complete the witness of God to His servants and messengers.

II. Accordingly, in discussing and estimating the credibility of *particular* miracles, instead of saying "miracles never happen" we should consider the nature and adequacy of the testimony to them; and also the adequacy of their moral purpose, and of their result.

Acceptance of the truth of the Resurrection practically involves the acceptance of the Incarnation and the Ascension.[2]

Consider next other arguments bearing on the miracles recorded in the Life of Jesus.[3]

(1) If the Synoptic Gospels (or any one of them) were published between 60 and 80 A.D., contemporaries of Jesus would be surviving, and such circumstantial accounts could hardly gain acceptance.

(2) Jesus's teaching (universally accepted

---

[1] See p. 151 ff.   [2] Goodwin, p. 271.
[3] Godet, p. 122 ff.

as authentic) is so closely interwoven with miracles that it is not possible to accept the one and reject the other. Jesus Himself, in His discourses, constantly appeals to His " works " as evidences of His Divine mission (Matthew xii. 22 ; John vi., ix.).

(3) Compare the simplicity of the Gospel records with the amazing fabrications of the Apocryphal Gospels, which show the character of purely human inventions in that age, even with the Gospels as models.

(4) The general argument from the analogy of the will of man is applicable *a fortiori* to the will of Him who came to reveal the Father, being one with Him in purpose.

(5) The circumstances that introduced and attended our Lord's earthly ministry make it antecedently probable that His mission would be attested by miracles.

(6) If belief is refused to these miracles of Jesus, the historical Christ disappears. What account then is to be given of that which actually came to pass, the immediate results of the preaching of the Gospel of the Resurrection; the conversion of the Roman world; " Christianity and Christendom " ?[1]

Destructive arguments are comparatively

---

[1] A. B. Bruce, chap. x.

easy (see Archbishop Whately's amusing proof of the non-existence of Napoleon Bonaparte); their weakness may often be shown by demanding a constructive account of that which is admitted to exist.

(7) The net result of criticism has been to show (*not*, as was argued in the Paulus-Strauss-Baur period, that the occurrence of miracle in a document is a proof of its late date and lack of authenticity, but) that the earliest documents contained a large proportion of miraculous records.[1]

Other considerations bearing on this subject will be found in a later section, on the character of Jesus.[2]

III. A more difficult question follows: Are the foregoing arguments valid in respect of every miracle recorded in the Bible? Plainly, while some retain their force *mutatis mutandis*, others are wholly or partially irrelevant.[3]

In the case of many of the Old Testament miracles the indications of adequate moral purpose are less convincing, and the testimony is not so strong. Accordingly, such narratives as the miracles wrought by Samson, and some of those attributed to Elisha, are

---

[1] A. B. Bruce, p. 110.   [2] See p. 151 ff.
[3] Archbishop Trench, *Miracles*, chap. iv. § 1.

the sport of secularist lecturers and other illiterate critics of the Bible. They base their criticisms on the assumption that Christian believers hold that every part of the Bible is inspired in the same degree. This view of inspiration, once common, has of late been largely modified; almost all Biblical scholars now recognise various grades of inspiration in the Bible books.[1]

Many questions respecting the date, the method of composition, the authenticity and authority of parts of the Old Testament are still under discussion; but the belief of most educated Christians in the truth of Christianity would not be in any way undermined by proof (if such were possible) that some of the Old Testament miracles were not supported by sufficient testimony to make them accepted as historical facts.[2] Professor Lias, in his *Principles of Biblical Criticism*, p. 217, says: "To demand as a condition precedent to the acceptance of Christianity that men shall first of all accept all the most startling miracles related in the Old Testament is, it may be granted, even a more dangerous course than that taken by

---

[1] Chap. IV.
[2] Archbishop Temple's *Bampton Lectures* (1884), *Religion and Science*, p. 153.

those who would make something like a clean sweep of them. . . . Even if we attempt to explain these miracles by natural causes, or imagine them to be in some cases merely the forms in which spiritual mysteries are presented to the untutored understanding, at least we need not shrink from the assertion that the finger of God is plainly manifested in the series of marvellous events related in the Old Testament."

And with regard to the more important miracles of the Old Testament it may be observed that they cluster round two critical epochs in the history of Israel, the establishment of the Theocracy under Moses and Joshua, and the restoration of the Theocracy through Elijah; at such times Jehovah's intervention to help His people was antecedently probable.[1] Much that has been said on p. 142 ff. is applicable to the miracles of these periods, as attestations and "signs." Of the miracles that preceded the Exodus it is said in the *Speaker's Commentary* (Introduction to vol. i.) that they are all, except the death of the first-born, specially Egyptian in character, corresponding to natural phenomena which frequently

---

[1] *Modern Scepticism* (Christian Evidence Society's Lectures, 1871).

happen, and occurring in their natural seasons.

Two recent expressions of opinion on this subject by distinguished scholars may be helpful.

Mr. Gladstone makes some valuable remarks on miracles in his *Studies on Bishop Butler*, p. 311 *sq*. Discussing Hume's argument, he refers to J. H. Newman's short but effective answer in the *Grammar of Assent*, p. 298; adding that, whereas Hume appeals to our experience of this uniformity of the "laws" of nature, our knowledge of these "laws" is obviously incomplete and progressive; it cannot be the basis of a general negation. We may admit that in the present state of knowledge miracles are "anomalies" in nature; but there is good reason for such anomalies, because miracles have served with great, perhaps indispensable power, in establishing the Jewish and Christian religions, whose great purpose is the "ejection of sin" from the world. He appeals to the analogy of the human will to God's action, in using, combining, modifying "laws" of nature for definite purposes. The denial of God's power or will to work miracles, because we conceive that experience is against it, is open to all the objections against Deism.

In *St. Paul the Traveller*, p. 87, Professor W. Ramsay says, "The marvels in Acts are difficulties, but the narrative apart from them is stamped as authentic, and they are an integral part of it. Twenty years ago I found it easy to dispose of them; nowadays probably not even the youngest among us can maintain that we have mastered the secrets of nature, and determined the limits that divide the unknown from the impossible. That Paul believed himself to be the recipient of direct revelations from God, to be guided and controlled in his plans by direct interpositions of the Holy Spirit, to be enabled by the Divine Power to move the forces of nature in a way that ordinary men cannot, is involved in this narrative. You must accept or reject it, but you cannot cut out the marvellous from the rest, or believe that either Paul or Luke was a mere victim of hallucinations. The marvellous is indissolubly interwoven with the narrative, and cannot be eliminated." It may be added that throughout the book Professor Ramsay shows his appreciation of St. Luke's ability and accuracy as a historian.

C.—The Character and Teaching of Jesus Christ as Evidences of His Divinity [1]

The main points to be noted are:—

(1) The impressions produced on His contemporaries; Pilate; the Roman centurion; the Apostles, especially John, Peter, and Judas.

(2) And on many moderns who have disbelieved His divinity, *e.g.* Strauss, Renan, Napoleon I.,[2] etc.

(3) His own unconsciousness of sin, "Which of you convinceth me of sin?" John viii. 46; "The prince of this world cometh, and hath nothing in me," xiv. 30; "I do always the things that are pleasing to the Father," viii. 29. He claims to be a ransom from sin, Mark x. 45; to be the judge of sinners, Matt. vii. 21-23.[3] In this respect the moral consciousness of Jesus differs not in degree only, but *in kind* from that of the best and holiest men, Socrates, Marcus Aurelius, even St. Paul

---

[1] Godet, *Defence of the Faith*, chap. v.; H. P. Liddon, *Bampton Lectures*, III. IV.

[2] Goodwin, p. 434.

[3] See Keim's summary of this argument quoted by Godet, p. 246.

and St. John (1 John i. 8, " If we say that we have no sin. . . .)

(4) His claims to divine power, as the Bread of life, John vi. 35; the Light of the world, viii. 12; the Son of Man (a most significant expression, see particularly Matt. xxvi. 63-65, and the parallels in Mark and Luke); equal to the Father, John v. 22, 23; one with the Father, John x. 30.[1] Other founders of a religion—Confucius, Zoroaster, Buddha—made no similar claims to a divine commission, with the exception of Moses (whose claim was attested by miracles and by results) and Mohammed.

(5) By the side of such claims set the traits of character universally recognised in Him; sincerity, and the demand for it in others (the Scribes and Pharisees, the rich young man); unselfishness, and requirement of it in others; humility, "I am meek and lowly in heart," Matt. xi. 29; and dislike of notoriety, Matt. xii. 16; ix. 30, etc.

The conclusion must be either—

that Jesus was a self-deluded fanatic, as his relatives thought at first, Mark iii. 21; and his enemies, John x. 20; this alternative,

---

[1] See the summary of these claims in Dr. G. P. Fisher's *Grounds of Theistic and Christian Belief*, p. 125.

adopted by Renan, demands explanations so forced and inconsistent that it is plainly a *reductio ad absurdum*;[1]

or that he was guilty of fraudulent imposture, an opinion open to even greater objections, and now generally scouted;

or that such claims and traits combined in one person are evidences of His divinity, and His sinlessness is a direct attestation of his "supernatural" mission; it is a "moral miracle" of the highest order.[2]

(6) The teaching of Jesus.

He is the only teacher who fully satisfies the needs and aspirations of human nature :[3]

(*a*) by His revelation of God as a Father;

(*b*) by His doctrine of salvation from the guilt and power of sin, thus satisfying a need felt by all races, and evidenced by sacrifice and other forms of propitiation. The Epistle to the Hebrews recognises the inefficacy of these, even in Judaism.

(*c*) Hence arose a new possibility of holiness in man, and a new standard of morality, which has regenerated human society

---

[1] Dr. Fisher, p. 178.
[2] See Professor A. B. Bruce, *The Miraculous Elements in the Gospels*, chaps. ix. x.
[3] *Modern Scepticism*, p. 429 (Christian Evidence Society's Lectures, 1871).

in proportion as it has been received and practised.[1]

(*d*) Jesus offers a new source of consolation for suffering and sorrow ("My peace I give unto you"): no other form of religion offers similar consolation; contrast the sadness of Stoicism in Marcus Aurelius, and the apathetic hopelessness of Buddhism.

(*e*) Jesus brings new hopes by His revelation of the Resurrection, the future life, the kingdom of heaven.

(7) The accuracy of historical detail which modern criticism has verified.

Add the fact that the history and character of Jesus, such as we know them, were accepted as historical within a few years by widely separated Churches in Asia, Greece, Syria, Italy, etc., as is seen from St. Paul's Epistles. Further, take into account the good sense, moderation, caution, and discretion shown by the leaders of the Church in its beginnings.

All that precedes rests on the assumption that the Jesus of the Gospels is historical. It may be well to say a word about the theory that the history and character of Jesus are largely "mythical," the product of gradual

[1] C. L. Brace, *Gesta Christi*.

accretions. On this assumption the unique and perfect character of Jesus is developed in four narratives, compiled from a mass of traditions, legends, myths, hallucinations, and pious fictions.[1] The fabricators and compilers of these materials must then have been persons of real genius and moral elevation; "the inventor of a Gospel would be a more astonishing character than the hero"; yet by hypothesis they were also credulous and superstitious enthusiasts.[2]

Now (even if we leave St. John aside, and consider only the synoptic Gospels) there seems to be insuperable difficulty in reconciling the supposed variety and multiplicity of origin and authorship with the unity, harmony, and perfection of the result, shown in the blending of Divine and human elements in Jesus Christ; the combination of love and beneficence with sternness; the mixture of humility with self-assertion; the creation of a new type of moral perfectness utterly unlike any in the past, or in the Gospel age; especially by the delineation of a suffering Messiah.[3]

[1] C. A. Row, *Christian Evidences*, chaps. iv. v. ; see also *Modern Scepticism*, p. 344 ff.
[2] Compare the Apocryphal Gospels.
[3] C. A. Row, *Christian Evidences*, p. 87 ff.

It is said by Dr. Keim (quoted in Fisher,[1] p. 173): "This mythical theory, which has lately become popular, is only a hypothesis, which explains some things, but does not explain the main thing; nay, deals with the historical facts from perverse and untenable points of view."

D. THE EVIDENTIAL VALUE OF ST. PAUL'S EPISTLES

It might seem natural, in connection with the character and teaching of Jesus, further to discuss the authority of the Gospels which give the portraiture of Him. But the discussion is long, complicated, full of unavoidable detail; moreover, the materials are easily accessible in such books as Bishop Westcott's *Introduction to the Study of the Gospels*, Bishop Ellicott's *Commentary*, the *Speaker's Commentary*, etc.

Also several of St. Paul's most important Epistles are earlier in date than the Gospels, whose authority is strongly reinforced by them. We have to consider—

---

[1] See also the summary in Row's *Christian Evidences*, chap. x. ; and in *Modern Scepticism*, p. 359.

I. *St. Paul's Value as a Witness*

(1) His authentic writings prove his great ability, and other intellectual qualities:

(2) also moral qualities necessary in a good witness, such as sincerity, toleration, calmness of judgment, accuracy (see Paley's *Horae Paulinae*).

(3) By training and position he was prejudiced against Jesus: he ascribes his conversion to a miracle. The theory which ascribes it to hallucination has been fairly described as "a cobweb of conjectures belied by the facts of the narrative." St. Paul claims to have actually seen and heard Jesus, and puts the appearance on a level with those seen by other apostles (1st Corinthians xv. 8; ix. 1). From Jesus Himself he claims to have received his commission.

(4) His sudden and absolute change of life and aims occurred when he was in fullest activity as a persecuting inquisitor; he then gave up everything, and proved his sincerity by life-long toils and sufferings.[1]

(5) He had easy access to the facts about Jesus and His Gospel. The date of his conversion was probably not later than 36 A.D.,

---

[1] Dean Farrar's *St. Paul*.

when he was still a young man; he had settled at Jerusalem soon after 30 A.D.; he must then have had full opportunity of learning the facts of Jesus's life, at any rate of His ministry in Judaea. Four of his chief epistles (Romans, 1st and 2nd Corinthians, Galatians), universally recognised as authentic after long discussion, were written probably in 57 or 58 A.D., less than thirty years after the Crucifixion.[1]

II. *Nature and Value of the Evidence supplied by the Epistles*

(1) When 1 Corinthians xv. 6 was written the larger number of 500 persons still survived who had seen Jesus after His resurrection. The same chapter shows that Paul's assertions about this and other appearances were already familiar to the Corinthians. Some of them were adversaries of Paul, some sceptical; they were keen-witted Greeks. If Paul's statements had been untrue, he would have been refuted, and certainly would not have written the 2nd Epistle to Corinthians.

(2) In Romans xv. 23 he says, "These

---

[1] C. A. Row, *Christian Evidences;* Professor Stanley Leathes in *Modern Scepticism,* p. 366.

many years I have a longing to come to you." He appeals to their knowledge (not learned from him) of the risen Christ as a living power, i. 3, 4 ; vi. 10 ; viii. 11 ; *i.e.* in Italy, as in Greece, when Paul wrote, less than thirty years after the Crucifixion, there was an identical belief in the risen Christ, which had already existed for some time.

(3) And further, we find in these Epistles a system of belief, such as we have it, about the Incarnation (Romans i. 3); Baptism (Romans vi. 3 ; 1 Corinthians i. 13 ; Galatians iii. 27); the Holy Communion (1 Corinthians xi. 23); etc.[1]

Further evidence of a similar kind might be adduced from other books of the New Testament, but the line of argument has perhaps been indicated sufficiently. It may be traced further by help of the ordinary commentaries.

E.—Christianity and Evolution

Having adduced certain evidences for Christianity based mainly on admitted facts, it may be well to consider some objections to

---

[1] See further remarks on the force of this evidence of Christian belief held firmly amid persecution in Row's *Christian Evidences*, p. 167 ; *Modern Scepticism*, pp. 401 *sq.*

Christianity, which are also said to rest upon admitted facts.

In many scientific and speculative works the theory of evolution is said to be fatal to Christian belief, and even to a belief in a Creator and moral Governor of the world, *i.e.* to religion. Evolution is defined as a theory "that all forms of life have been evolved or developed from simple and low organisms, and that in the long series of successive developments each organism tended continually to develop into more complex forms, and organs that at first had several functions tended to become specialised."[1] With this theory is closely connected Darwin's theory of natural selection, and the "struggle for existence."

Now this theory or hypothesis (so far as it is scientifically proved) appears to be quite compatible not only with religion, but with the Christian religion.

(1) It has, no doubt, modified the form of the "argument from design" (the teleological argument) which is prominent in such books as Paley's *Natural Theology*, the *Bridgwater Treatises*, etc.; viz. that the facts of nature, especially the animal creation, give innumerable proofs of a Creator and

[1] Cassell's *Dictionary*.

Designer of Nature; and show His power, wisdom, and goodness by the ways in which parts of the organism (such as the eye or the hand) are adapted to external circumstances,[1] and to particular purposes;[2] whereas the evolution theory ascribes these appearances of design, not to the creation of definite species of plants, animals, etc., by separate creative acts;[3] but to the slow continuous action of natural forces and "laws," such as heredity, variation, influences of environment, combined with "natural selection," which have winnowed out such variations in species and individuals as were less favourable, and developed such as were more favourable to life; so that the eye, for instance, is but a highly developed form of some rudimentary organ, or even of a mere cell. Similarly man himself is said to be developed from lower stages of existence, and even the whole solar system to be developed from a mass of heated nebulous matter.[4]

This theory, however, does not affect the

---

[1] Paley's *Natural Theology*, chaps. iii. vi.
[2] For a short summary of the argument, and of its history, see Dr. R. Flint's *Theism*, pp. 196, 387.
[3] Milton, *Paradise Lost*, vii. 414.
[4] For a sketch of Laplace's and Darwin's theories see Archbishop Temple's *Bampton Lectures*, p. 163 *sq.*; Flint, *Theism*, pp. 200, 397.

substance of the "argument from design," but only its details, and the way of putting it. In fact, the proofs of the power, wisdom, and goodness of God become even stronger than before, if the latent properties of matter, and the forces that act upon it, were devised by God in such a way as to produce by their mutual action in the course of ages all the wonders of nature, including man. Further, matter and force cannot act of themselves; so that the theory of evolution implies God's "immanence in nature, and the constant omnipresence of His shaping and directing power."[1]

(2) How does the theory affect belief in the Bible, and especially in the narratives of Creation given in Genesis? Science has filled in with magnificent wealth of accurate detail the rudimentary traditional outlines of the Bible record; and it has been said previously[2] that the Bible record is not intended as a Divine revelation of scientific facts; in particular as to the antiquity of man on the earth Genesis gives no certain date. On the other hand, Darwin's theory of man's origin and development is still imperfectly proved.

Is there any valid objection against the

---

[1] Aubrey Moore, *Science and the Faith*, p. 184.
[2] Chap. IV.

hypothesis that at a certain stage in the evolution of the world, so soon as certain conditions were satisfied, a new "law," brought into operation by the Divine initiative, was manifested by the development of the "supersensual" phenomena of consciousness, the sense of duty, and all the special powers and qualities of the human soul?[1] This would be analogous to what happened at the introduction into the world, first of life in its lower forms; then of feeling, instinct, etc.

(3) The theory of evolution itself supplies an answer to objections against God's power, wisdom, and goodness based on the existence of pain and suffering and on the apparent waste of life; viz. that in a work which *ex hypothesi* is still unfinished, there necessarily must be imperfections, which must be inexplicable to those who cannot see the ultimate issue.[2]

F.—EVOLUTION IN HISTORY

History, showing the course of God's designs for the development and education of mankind,

[1] A. R. Wallace, *Darwinism*, last chapter.
[2] *Lux Mundi*, p. 190. (See in *Modern Scepticism*, p. 259 *sq.*, a lecture by Bishop Goodwin on the lines of Butler's *Analogy*, respecting the analogy between evolution in Nature, and evolution in Revelation.)

strongly corroborates the teachings of Revelation. It shows "God in history,"[1] preparing the world for Jesus Christ, so that Augustine boldly says, "Christianity is as old as the world"; Christ came in the fulness of time, as the consummation of ages of moral, social, and political evolution. This slow process was strictly analogous to the slow development of Nature. The main lines of converging progress can be traced in the history of Greece, Rome, and the Jewish race.

(*a*) In Greece, guarded against Asiatic despotism by the spirit of Athens and Sparta, against the uncivilised powers of the North and West by its mountain rampart and the sea, the flower and fruit of Hellenic civilisation had time to come to perfection before Macedon and Rome had strength to hinder it.

Thus were developed (1) the highest type of human excellence in literature, art, etc.,[2] which yet showed man's incapacity to solve unaided the "enigmas of life," and to discover truth and righteousness; (2) the cultivation of the reasoning faculty and power of dialectic, which, though in pre-Christian times incapable

---

[1] Bishop of Rochester in *Lux Mundi*; Dean Farrar's Hulsean Lectures (1870), the *Witness of History to Christ*.
[2] Archbishop Temple, *Essays and Reviews*, p. 15 ff.

of arriving at religious truth, yet was invaluable to the early Church for winnowing truth from falsehood; (3) a perfect language, which became the vehicle of revelation in the LXX. and New Testament, being spread widely over the East through Alexander's conquests.

(*b*) Rome developed and handed on (1) traditions and examples of stern, manly virtues; fortitude, austere simplicity, patriotism, and public spirit: (2) a framework of law and political organisation which was of immense value in the development of the Church both in the East and the West: (3) the "Pax Romana," giving physical, material, and moral facilities for the spread of Christianity; in the Acts may be seen the helpfulness of the imperial provincial system, established not long before the foundation of the Church:[1] (4) some elements of "moral preparation" in the Stoic philosophy.[2]

(*c*) The Jewish nation and race present evidences of evolution in the Law, prophecy, and history.[3]

(1) The Law—its sacrifices, in themselves ineffectual, pointing forward to their "fulfilment"

---

[1] Professor Ramsay's books (*passim*).
[2] Dean Farrar's *Seekers after God*.
[3] C. A. Row's *Christian Evidences*, chap. xi.

in Christ; its ritual, whose symbolism was fulfilled in Christ; its morality, progressively training the Jewish people, and "fulfilled" by Christ; its progressive religious teaching on the unity and holiness of God, on the destiny of man, and his obligation to seek righteousness from a higher source.[1]

(2) The Prophets. In Paley and other older books undue importance is attached to the more or less literal fulfilment of predictive prophecy, especially in reference to the Messiah. Lists of these are given in many accessible books.[2] The argument still has a certain weight, for the conditions of a weighty prophecy are often satisfied, viz. that it should be "obscure when delivered, clear when fulfilled" (for if clear when delivered, it is liable to the objection that it had traced the lines for its own fulfilment); and the fulfilment in Jesus Christ of many apparently incompatible prophecies is like finding the right key for a complicated lock. Moreover, from Abraham to Malachi there is a continuous series of prophets whose "collective consciousness" is a cumulative argument of enormous weight, and

---

[1] Bishop Westcott, *Ep. to Hebrews;* Fisher's *Christian Belief,* p. 405.
[2] Whately's *Evidences,* chap. iv.; Chalmers's *Evidences,* p. 180.

little affected by questions about the date and authorship of individual books. No one disputes that all the books in which prophecies occur were in existence, and accepted by the Jews, long before Christ. It may be added that, however numerous and convergent, these prophecies would have been utterly insufficient of themselves for constructing the portrait of Christ as given in the Gospels.[1]

Yet, after all, "the fulfilment of prophecy is an obscure and difficult subject; the safety of Christian truth should not be made to depend much upon it."[2] There is another view of prophecy which displays more clearly its permanent value and importance. The prophets educated their race in great religious ideas; monotheism; the government of the world by a just and holy God; a Divine purpose shaping the history of nations,[3] and preparing by slow steps the advent of a new kingdom of righteousness, arising in and from Israel, yet admitting all nations into it (Jer. xxxi. 31-34; Isaiah lvi. 7; lx.; Hebrews viii. 8-13). Much of their teaching was, no

---

[1] On the evidential force of predictive prophecy see C. A. Row, *Bampton Lectures*, 1877, p. 219, etc.; Bishop Westcott on *Hebrews*, p. 69.
[2] Goodwin, p. 134.
[3] Bunsen, *God in History*, p. 140.

doubt, rudimentary and embryonic; in this it resembled other evolutionary developments; but it had this special mark of "supernatural" force, that the prophet is often utterly opposed to the spirit of the time in which he lives, nay, shrinks himself from the message he delivers; and his message reaches beyond the facts and possibilities of the present, having not only a partial fulfilment at the time, but also "a germinant accomplishment through many ages," culminating in the kingdom of Christ.[1]

(3) The history of the Jews: evolved in successive stages, from the call of Abraham, and the promises, to the deliverance from Egypt; the long struggles against powerful idolatrous nations (during which their monotheism was braced and purified); the Exile and its chastening; the unique phenomenon of the Return; the Dispersion, scattering the Jews east and west, to carry with them their Scriptures, which powerfully helped the diffusion of Christianity.[2]

Yet it cannot be said that Christianity was simply a "natural" evolution from Judaism. These influences and forces had not prepared

---

[1] On the work of the prophets see also Chap. IV. p. 104; Professor W. Sanday, *Inspiration*, Lecture III.

[2] Godet, p. 199.

the leaders of Jewish thought, religion, and society to receive Christ; they crucified Him. Nevertheless God's preparation of "the remnant" had been effectual, and the crucified King of the Jews established the new kingdom of righteousness.

G.—CHRISTIANITY AND CHRISTENDOM

These are, as Coleridge said, two of the main evidences for the Gospel, meaning by this—

(1) The relations of Christian doctrines to human needs and aspirations; by their conformity with the voice of conscience ("Revelation is probable, not because the truths it makes known to us are distant, but because they are so near,"[1]) *cf.* Deuteronomy xxx. 11-14; by satisfying the need of something higher and larger than earth can give (Job xiv. 1; Ecclesiastes ii.); by solving the problems of suffering, pain, death, which baffle and sadden philosophic speculation; by releasing from the sense of guilt and fear, evidenced by the almost universal prevalence of sacrifice.[2] Christianity satisfies all these needs and aspirations by offering reconciliation to God

---

[1] Dr. H. Wace, *Boyle Lectures*, p. 264.
[2] Fisher, p. 338.

through a Saviour who, having borne our nature, knows our wants, brings pardon of sin, hope and consolation in sorrow, and deliverance from death, through union with the Divine nature, and progressive advance in the spiritual life, which is begun on earth, and perfected hereafter. By these offers, open to all men without distinction, it conquered Paganism in the first centuries, and has won the allegiance of the most highly civilised races.

There is much to be said also about the intellectual depth and strength of Christian philosophy, as compared with other philosophies, on such subjects as God, man, will, sin, pain, death, etc.;[1] a fresh evidence of "supernatural" influences acting on a handful of unlettered Jews in the first century.

(2) The effects of Christian doctrines on national and social development.

They show their vital power by supplying the motives and the means for continuous advance towards a high ideal; by teaching the equality of men, and thus undermining slavery; by raising the position of women; by stimulating philanthropy; by reconciling freedom of opinion with obedience to authority; by laying down

[1] Aubrey Moore in *Lux Mundi*.

principles which have already greatly influenced international and social relations, and seem destined to influence them still more; by encouraging missionary enterprise in all Christian Churches; and by raising the Christian nations above the moral and religious standard of the rest of the world, in proportion to the purity and sincerity of Christian belief and practice.[1]

(C. L. Brace, *Gesta Christi*, 1886, shows the influence of the Gospel during the Roman period on *patria potestas* and family relations, in checking unnatural vice and teaching purity, in putting an end to the exposure of children, in encouraging philanthropy and charitable institutions, in checking licentious and cruel sports, in promoting humane legislation, in mitigating and undermining slavery, in elevating marriage and the position of women.)

(3) The force of the foregoing considerations will be strengthened by a brief comparison between Christianity and the other great religions of the world.[2]

St. Paul (Romans ii. 14, 15; i. 19, 20)

---

[1] Fisher, p. 368 ff.
[2] Professor Max Müller, *Chips from a German Workshop*, vol. i.; C. Hardwick, *Christ and Other Masters*.

teaches us to regard them as more or less imperfect means of training the conscience, in so far as the followers of each religion are faithful to its highest principles. "There is no religion which, among its many errors, does not contain some divine truths" (St. Augustine). But they all lack the vitalising progressive powers of Christianity; they are stationary and stagnant, and therefore liable to deadly corruption. Paganism, comparatively pure in the Homeric age, ultimately sank into nameless abominations (Romans i. 21-32).

Besides Christianity and the innumerable varieties of savage religions, there are six great historical religions [1]—

(*a*) Semitic—(1) Judaism, superseded, as we believe, by Christianity;

(2) Mohammedanism, valuable by its antagonism to idolatry, its central doctrine of submission to the will of God, and its enforcement of certain moral virtues. But even those who most appreciate its good qualities insist on its inferiority to Christianity, in representing God not as Love, but as absolute arbitrary Will; in making access to God indirect, through the Prophet;

---

[1] Professor Max Müller, vol. iv.; F. D. Maurice, *Boyle Lectures*.

in its lower ideals of morality, holiness, and spiritual life; in appealing to lower motives, of fear, sensual desire, etc.; in the immeasurable inferiority of its sacred writings; and in its lack of progressiveness, largely due to the doctrine of "Kismet."[1]

(*b*) Aryan—(3) Brahmanism, which appears to be gradually collapsing under the influence of western ideas and missionary enterprise.

(4) The small remnant of Zoroaster's followers (said to be only about 100,000) are becoming subject to similar influences.

(5) Buddhism, numbering some 450 millions of adherents, has attracted attention and sympathy in the West by the life and character of its founder, "one of the most beautiful figures in Paganism, whose self-sacrifice might read a useful lesson to Christians";[2] by the elevation and purity of its moral teaching, far superior to Mohammedanism or Stoicism; by some singular resemblances to Christian systems; and by its pessimistic mysticism, which has had a strange charm for some European agnostics. But in the religion of Buddha there is no god; life

---

[1] Mr. R. Bosworth Smith, *Mohammedanism;* Stanley's *Eastern Church,* Lecture VIII.; Dr. R. Flint, *Theism.*
[2] H. P. Liddon, *Essays and Addresses.*

is a misery for soul and body, from which there is no escape but Nirvana, which is practically extinction; it inspires no idea of duty, and its mainspring is but a subtle form of selfishness.[1] In fact, it is not so much a religion as a philosophy of life; and therefore, like the doctrine of Socrates, in its purer form it attracts only the few; to the many it offers neither hope nor faith, and in its more prevalent forms it has degenerated by curious stages into external formalism and grovelling idolatry; while neither the old nor the new Buddhism profess to do much for practical morality.

(6) The sixth great religion is Confucianism.[2] Its founder (551-473 B.C.) made no claim to a divine mission; he taught no theology, but only a lofty, purely secular morality (possibly derived from the same sources as that of Pythagoras), based on the assumption of man's original purity and innocence.

> Superior and alone Confucius stood,
> Who taught that useful science, to be good.
> POPE.

One of his sayings was, "He only is pure in

---

[1] Sir Edwin Arnold, *The Light of Asia*; H. P. Liddon, *Essays and Addresses*; Bunsen, *God in History*, vol. i. p. 374; Bishop R. S. Copleston on *Buddhism in Ceylon*.

[2] General Alexander, *Life of Confucius*.

mind who hates vice as one would hate a bad odour." In its purer form Confucianism has an elevating influence, especially on the educated classes, but being merely secular, it fails to satisfy the deep-seated craving for religion. Accordingly, the bulk of the Chinese have turned either to idolatrous corruptions of Buddhism, or to the worship of ancestors.

Fuller study of the comparative history of Religions will deepen the conviction that Christianity differs from them all in *kind;* in its origin, in its "supernatural" sanctions confirmed by historical facts, in its ideal, in its accomplished results, and in its promise of the future.[1] "In Christ is life; and the life is the light of men."

H.—The Cumulative Value of these Evidences

It is a law of evidence that one witness to a fact or statement may be of little weight. Two or three independent witnesses may suffice for absolute proof; and if more independent witnesses are brought forward, the probability of the truth of their testimony

---

[1] S. T. Coleridge, *Aids to Reflection.*

increases, not in arithmetical, but more nearly in geometrical ratio.

Similarly, in proportion as Christian evidences are independent and trustworthy, their cumulative force is measured, not by addition, but by multiplication. The evidences here presented may be thus summarised—

(1) The manifest preparation for Christianity in history.

(2) The work of prophecy in foretelling and preparing.

(3) The historical facts concerning Jesus Christ.

(4) The witness of the several books of the New Testament, especially St. Paul's epistles and the Gospels, to the "supernatural" events of His earthly life. A century of criticism has in some respects greatly strengthened the cogency of this branch of the "evidences."

(5) The unique position, character, and teaching of Jesus.

(6) If the possibility and probability of Divine intervention for an adequate purpose be admitted, miracles supported by adequate historical testimony are strong evidences.

(7) The doctrines of Christianity and their historical results.

(8) (A branch of evidence which does not

by its nature admit of being formally set forth and discussed) the witness of the Holy Spirit to Christ in the individual conscience.

(9) His witness in the corporate life of Christ's Church.

I.—The Difficulties of Constructive Unbelief

There is little or no difficulty in taking up the position of destructive or negative unbelief. As religion has to do with the unseen, eternal, and infinite, it is naturally open to doubts and objections on the part of those who take their stand on what is seen, temporal, and limited, *i.e.* on facts of sense and experience, scientific evidence, etc.; and deny the existence of anything beyond. For meeting purely negative and destructive arguments the *method* of Bishop Butler's *Analogy* will supply some help; it has been ably used by Christian apologists.[1]

Again, there is no difficulty whatever in adopting the commoner form of " Agnosticism," which practically consists in taking unbelief on trust without inquiry. But it is not a position worthy of an educated man, who ought to care

[1] Mr. Gladstone's *Studies subsidiary to Butler's Analogy.*

to inquire what answers have been given to the great questions of human existence. It is, in fact, intellectually contemptible to take a lively interest about the last scrap of news in the evening paper, about a murder or a divorce scandal; and yet to care nothing, and inquire nothing about the evidence for the existence of a God, or the question whether Jesus Christ is the Son of God, or was an impostor or a fanatic. A million people of the ordinary "Agnostic" stamp, who take unbelief on trust from sheer intellectual laziness or frivolity, do not weigh in the scale against one convinced believer; or even against one unbeliever who, having done his best to explore the great questions of existence, honestly concludes that he can find no satisfactory solution.[1] But in regard to inquiring unbelievers Dr. Martineau says,[2] "To make the case of Agnosticism good, you must be

[1] "I should deem him a coward who did not prove to the uttermost what is said about such questions (life, death, immortality). He should persevere until he has attained one of two things; either he should discover or learn the truth about them; or, if this is impossible, I would have him take the best and most irrefragable of human notions, and let this be the raft on which he sails through life—not without risk, as I admit—if he cannot find some word of God which will more surely and safely carry him."—Plato, *Phaedo*, chap. xxxv. p. 85 (Jowett's translation).

[2] *Study of Religion*, preface, p. viii.

careful not to look beyond phenomena, as empirical facts; you must abjure the inquiry into causes, and the attempt to trace invisible issues, and never lift the veil that bounds experience. But if once you allow yourself to think about the origin and end of things, you will have to believe in a God and immortality."

By constructive unbelief is meant any non-Christian theory of human existence based upon inquiry into causes, and thoughts "about the origin and end of things." Such a theory has to take into its account, among these ideas and inquiries, the sense of obligation (that "ought" which Bentham wished to abolish); the sense of the Infinite; and the things that trouble human life—sin, pain, sorrow, death, as well as the apparent injustices and inequalities of life.

Besides Christianity and the other great religions, there are certain constructive theories or philosophies which attempt to give an account of these fundamental facts and difficulties of human existence; such as Pantheism; Dualism (of two co-ordinate powers of good and evil, an ancient theory which found an able modern advocate in J. S. Mill); forms of pessimistic philosophy reproducing some of the features of Buddhism; various forms of "Positive" philosophy, recognising nothing but matter and force; Herbert Spencer's "Unknowable, but omniscient and Eternal Power, the cause of all phenomena"; Matthew Arnold's shadowy "Power not ourselves" (and not personal) "that makes for righteousness"; and Theism in its various forms.[1]

There is another attempted solution, the reformed Christianity, which would eliminate all the "supernatural" and miraculous elements, and retain only the morality of Christianity. This is well dissected by Bishop Goodwin (*The Creed*, p. 449 *sq.*), who shows that though it retains some of the outward form of Christianity, it has no vital principle, no heart, blood, or life; no promise of endurance even in a sect, still less of becoming the basis of a world religion.[2]

Some of these systems explain away the sense of moral obligation; not one of them gives an adequate account of the "enigmas of

---

[1] Dr. J. Martineau, *Study of Religion*, vol. i.; *Types of Ethical Theory*, vol. ii.; Professor H. Sidgwick, *History of Ethics*.

[2] See also the chapter on "Christianity without Miracle" in Professor A. B. Bruce's *Miraculous Elements in the Gospels*. His conclusion is that "Christianity without miracle must cease to be a substantive religion."

life"; not one offers or supplies to ordinary men and women the strong sanctions of duty and morality; the comfort and strength in sorrow and pain; the release from the power, guilt, and misery of sin; the hope and courage in the face of death and bereavement; the trust in God's Fatherly love of the individual soul and of human kind, which Christianity offers through faith in Christ, and through the piety, worship, service, brotherhood, and fellowship with God and man, which are among the fruits of the Tree of Life that is for the healing of the nations (Rev. xxii. 2).[1]

"Lord, to whom shall we go? Thou hast the words of eternal life."

[1] See also section *G.—Christianity and Christendom.*

THE END

MACMILLAN AND CO.'S PUBLICATIONS.

AN INTRODUCTION TO THE STUDY OF THE GOSPELS. By BROOKE FOSS WESTCOTT, D.D., D.C.L., Lord Bishop of Durham, etc. Eighth Edition. Crown 8vo. 10s. 6d.

A GENERAL SURVEY OF THE HISTORY OF THE CANON OF THE NEW TESTAMENT DURING THE FIRST FOUR CENTURIES. By B. F. WESTCOTT, D.D., etc. Sixth Edition. Crown 8vo. 10s. 6d.

THE BIBLE IN THE CHURCH: a popular account of the collection and reception of the Holy Scriptures in the Christian Churches. By B. F. WESTCOTT, D.D., D.C.L. Pott 8vo. 4s. 6d.

DISSERTATIONS ON THE APOSTOLIC AGE. Reprinted from editions of St. Paul's Epistles. By J. B. LIGHTFOOT, D.D., LL.D., D.C.L., late Bishop of Durham. 8vo. 14s.

BIBLICAL ESSAYS. By J. B. LIGHTFOOT, D.D., etc. 8vo. 12s.

AN INTRODUCTION TO THE ARTICLES OF THE CHURCH OF ENGLAND. By the Rev. G. F. MACLEAR, D.D., and the Rev. W. W. WILLIAMS, M.A., formerly Vice-Principal of the Missionary College, Dorchester, Fellow of St. Augustine's College, Canterbury. Crown 8vo. 10s. 6d.

SELECTIONS FROM EARLY WRITERS. Illustrative of Church History to the Time of Constantine. By HENRY MELVILL GWATKIN, M.A., Dixie Professor of Ecclesiastical History in the University of Cambridge. Crown 8vo. 4s. net.

JUDAISTIC CHRISTIANITY. A Course of Lectures. By the late Rev. F. J. A. HORT, D.D. Crown 8vo. 6s.

SIX LECTURES ON THE ANTE-NICENE FATHERS. By the late Rev. F. J. A. HORT, D.D. Crown 8vo. 3s. 6d.

THE CHRISTIAN ECCLESIA. A Course of Lectures and Four Sermons. By the late Rev. F. J. A. HORT, D.D. Crown 8vo. 6s.

THE CANON OF THE OLD TESTAMENT. An Essay on the Growth and Formation of the Hebrew Canon of Scripture. By H. E. RYLE, D.D., Hulsean Professor of Divinity, Cambridge; Professorial Fellow of King's College, Cambridge; and Examining Chaplain to the Lord Bishop of Ripon. Second Edition. Crown 8vo. 6s.

THE EARLY NARRATIVES OF GENESIS. A Brief Introduction to the Study of Genesis I.-XI. By H. E. RYLE, D.D., etc. Crown 8vo. 3s. net.

THE DIVINE LIBRARY OF THE OLD TESTAMENT. Its Origin, Preservation, Inspiration, and Permanent Value. Five Lectures by A. F. KIRKPATRICK, D.D., Regius Professor of Hebrew in the University of Cambridge, and Canon of Ely. Crown 8vo. 3s. net.

THE DOCTRINE OF THE PROPHETS. The Warburtonian Lectures for 1886-1890. By A. F. KIRKPATRICK, D.D. Second Edition. Crown 8vo. 6s.

MACMILLAN AND CO., LTD., LONDON.

MACMILLAN AND CO.'S PUBLICATIONS.

THE COMPOSITION OF THE FOUR GOSPELS. A critical inquiry. By the Rev. ARTHUR WRIGHT, M.A., Fellow and Tutor of Queen's College, Cambridge. Crown 8vo. 5s.

THE COMMON TRADITION OF THE SYNOPTIC GOSPELS IN THE TEXT OF THE REVISED VERSION. By EDWIN A. ABBOTT, D.D., formerly Fellow of St. John's College, Cambridge, and W. G. RUSHBROOKE, M.L., formerly Fellow of St. John's College, Cambridge. Crown 8vo. 3s. 6d.

THE CENTRAL TEACHING OF CHRIST. Being a Study and Exposition of St. John, Chapters xiii.-xvii. inclusive. By T. D. BERNARD, M.A., Canon and Chancellor of Wells. Crown 8vo. 7s. 6d.

THE LEADING IDEAS OF THE GOSPELS. By the Right Rev WILLIAM ALEXANDER, D.D., Bishop of Derry and Raphoe. New Edition, revised and enlarged. Crown 8vo. 6s.

A HISTORY OF THE CHRISTIAN CHURCH DURING THE FIRST SIX CENTURIES. By S. CHEETHAM, D.D., F.S.A., Archdeacon and Canon of Rochester, Honorary Fellow of Christ's College, Cambridge, Fellow and Emeritus Professor of King's College, London. Crown 8vo. 10s. 6d.

OUTLINES OF CHURCH HISTORY. By RUDOLF SOHM, Professor of Law, Leipzig. Translated by Miss MAY SINCLAIR. With a preface by Professor H. M. GWATKIN. Crown 8vo. 3s. 6d.

A CLASS-BOOK OF OLD TESTAMENT HISTORY. By the Rev. G. F. MACLEAR, D.D., Warden of St. Augustine's College, and Honorary Canon of Canterbury, late Head Master of King's College School, author of "The Evidential Value of the Holy Eucharist," etc. With maps. Pott 8vo. 4s. 6d.

A CLASS-BOOK OF NEW TESTAMENT HISTORY. By the Rev. G. F. MACLEAR, D.D., etc. With maps. Pott 8vo. 5s. 6d.

AN INTRODUCTION TO THE CREEDS. By the Rev. G. F MACLEAR, D.D. Pott 8vo. 3s. 6d.

AN ELEMENTARY INTRODUCTION TO THE BOOK OF COMMON PRAYER. By the Rev. FRANCIS PROCTER, M.A., Vicar of Witton, Norfolk; author of "A History of the Book of Common Prayer," and the Rev. G. F. MACLEAR, D.D., Warden of St. Augustine's College, and Honorary Canon of Canterbury, late Head Master of King's College School. Pott 8vo. 2s. 6d.

MACMILLAN AND CO., LTD., LONDON.

www.ingramcontent.com/pod-product-compliance
Lightning Source LLC
Chambersburg PA
CBHW032133160426
43197CB00008B/623